Cognitive Behavioral Therapy (CBT):

Techniques for Retraining Your Brain and Managing Depression and Anxiety in Just 7 Weeks or Less

Table of Contents

Introduction ──────────────────────── i

Chapter 1: Relationship Factors When it Comes to CBT ──────────────────────── 1

   The Role of the Therapist ─────────── 2

   Expertise vs. Equality ──────────────── 3

   Coping as Opposed to Mastery ──────── 8

   The Utilization of Self-Disclosure ───────── 9

   Meta-Cognition ──────────────────── 13

Chapter2: Problems Faced by Individuals Who Seek Help in Cognitive Behavioral Therapy ── 15

   Disadvantages of Cognitive Behavioral Therapy ────────────────────────── 21

Chapter3: How CBT Works in a Holistic Manner ───────────────────────────── 23

   Value of Cognitive Behavioral Therapy ──── 26

   Changing Perceptions and Distortions ──── 27

   The Stages of Cognitive Behavioral Therapy ─────────────────────────── 29

   What to Expect ─────────────────── 30

   Understanding YourThoughts ─────────── 31

   Behavior Stage ─────────────────── 33

   Learning Stage ─────────────────── 34

Chapter 4: Intrusive Thoughts and How to Deal with Them — 36

How to Identify the Negative Automatic Thoughts — 39

How to Cope with Unwanted Thoughts — 40

Cognitive Behavioral Techniques for Intrusive Thoughts — 42

- Scheduling Positive Activities — 43
- Hierarchy of Concerns — 43
- Thought Records — 44
- The Stop Technique — 49
- Stress Inoculation Approaches — 50

CBT and Spirituality — 51

Is Spirituality Relevant When It Comes to CBT — 52

Religious Models Concerning the Mind — 53

- Islam — 54
- Christianity — 54

CBT and Spirituality in Practice — 60

Joint Workings — 62

Beliefs — 63

Spiritually based CBT is effective for depression — 66

Fostering good spirituality — 69

Spirituallly Integrated Treatment ----------- 72

Chapter5: Benefits of Cognitive Behavioral Therapy --- 79

1. It can be used in place of medication - 79
2. Time efficiency --------------------------- 82
3. Flexibility -------------------------------- 83
4. Collaborative approach --------------- 85
5. Structured nature ----------------------- 87
6. Skills and strategies ------------------- 89
7. Support --------------------------------- 91
8. Self-Esteem --------------------------- 93
9. Change of thought ------------------- 95
10. Anger management ------------------ 97
11. Communication skills ---------------- 99
12. Coping skills ------------------------- 101
13. Preventing relapse ------------------ 102
14. Addiction --------------------------- 104
15. Anxiety ----------------------------- 106
16. Depression ------------------------- 107

Chapter 6: Most optimal CBT practices ----- 110

1. Journaling ----------------------------- 110
2. Behavioral Experiments --------------- 111
3. Pleasurable activities ----------------- 113

4. Situation-exposure hierarchies----- 114
5. Imagery-based exposure -------------- 115
6. Cognitive restructuring-------------- 116
7. Socratic questioning ------------------- 118
8. Relaxed breathing ------------------- 119
9. Statements to counteract the negative 120
10. Progressive muscle relaxation (PMR) 122

Conclusion ------------------------------------- 123

Introduction

Different factors affect our feelings and behaviors as individuals and this, in turn, shapes us into the people we become. Cognitive Behavioral Therapy is a field of psychotherapy which considers an individual's mental framework i.e. their beliefs, attitudes towards things and their perception and understanding (thoughts) influence their feelings and behaviors. The point of this is to aid people to have better ways of reacting to different stimuli (situations) in their life. These are habitual things that are instilled, and they come in handy when it comes to releasing your mental and physical condition which, in turn, allows people to have better attitudes.

Everyone has problems and these are from the scenarios we face in our environment. Every day we meet new people with different attitudes towards us or we solve new challenges that were not there before or even face different social situations we had not experienced before. As human beings, we draw something from this, we draw meaning, and that affects or forms our attitudes towards these different scenarios. it shapes our attitudes and behaviors as stated before, and that's where Cognitive Behavioral Therapy comes into play. It helps us correctly interpret and assess our situations and so guides us on the proper way to react to the situations.

Cognitive Behavioral Therapy is structured so that there is an instructor or counselor that leads the regular meetings and the issues addressed vary from social too emotional in a series of agenda or topic-based meetings.

These meetings deal with:

Defining the issue clearly, the counselor helps the patient find out what the issue of concern is and by doing so assists them to gain clarity of where they stand and the depth of the subject matter or issue of concern.After this, the counselor helps the student construct a framework of meaning that is, a thought pattern around the issues he or she is facing this helps the patient understand what he or she is feeling and why they are feeling that way. It's a gradual process as the instructor does not coach the patient on what to think. Rather you are being guided on the ways to assess yourself and the work of the therapist is to help you arrive at this goal.

The next thing is the counselor would assist you to consider whether or not the assessments drawn on the situation are wrong or misguided and you would not let them down at this point as the third party opinion would be telling you whether your assumptions are wrong or right. If they are wrong that takes us to the next step here the instructor helps you lay out what the truth is(facts) and he or she helps you distinguish this from what is made up(irrational thoughts) at this point where are taking nothing for granted and we are making knowledgeable and decisions with clarity in place.

From that point, the counselor now helps the patient through carrying out a case study to try and figure out if this is the first time this situation has occurred and if it is not how the situation was handled the first time it occurred. People have a tendency of being consistent with their attitudes towards stimuli. What that means is that if someone hurt you once most of us carry it with us and if it ever happens again they would validate their behavior by pointing out their experiences. The counselor would help you address this and clear your mind of those thoughts and try and help you treat every situation independently and make you see everything as is without a clouded judgment.

The next part of the session is aimed at coming up with a solution to the problem. Here we are well on our way to making the correct decision or behavior towards the situation. The counselor advised seeing a good outcome and positivity out of everything and stops looking forward to the negatives or the worst outcome possible from the situation. People have the tendency of making poor choices and decisions in life because of the fear of the outcome. Failure and other people image of us has taken the forefront and people are losing themselves to poor life choices because of fear of negative outcomes being too focused on what can go wrong that's why people do not go into business, stay in bad relationships and even take on career paths they do not feel.

The counselor then goes to the next step which is showing the patient a different side or perspective to the one he or she currently sees. This is basically giving them a wider range of situations to draw conclusions from and it allows the patient to make a decision coming from a point of knowledge and the behavior will reflect his understanding and his maturity towards the handling of the situations.

From this point, we now look at a social part of the cognitive behavioral theory. The counselor then helps his client make meaning out of human behavior and actions, the point of this is to help the patient understand that whatever happened is a reaction to certain stimuli and is not necessarily a direct attack against them. People go through a lot and this affects them mentally and emotionally and at times they carry this burden through the night and into the day and react to you negatively without really meaning to or some have been through situations that have instilled a certain mentality within them and it affects their actions and behaviors. Understanding this about people will help clear your preexisting assumptions and beliefs about the situation and help you make a just decision or behavior.

The next phase involves mentality and perception; here the counselor puts an emphasis on positive thinking always assuming the best always wanting the best. From every situation and challenges faced, there should be the assumption the best will come out of it. Drawing positives from everything which is possible can help us make decisions without fearing for the worst.

The next session is being conscious of your own feelings or mood. This will help you be in control. Most times, our mood affects how we react to things. We overreact because of bad moods and let things slide because of good moods. Having control of one's emotions will ensure that we are in control of our behavior. We can avoid making hasty decisions we later regret due to anger and also take time to think things over before making decisions which ensure that the decision made or behavior shown towards something is the right one at all times.

The next thing in the course of the therapy is the nature of the goals we set for ourselves. Most of the time or almost all the time people will tell you they want to do big things and have a big impact. They may want power, money, and success and they want it fast. The downside is that they do not know or do not care about the work it takes to get there and they are misguided by social media into thinking they are not enough or worth and this affects them mentally and emotionally. The setting of realistic and attainable goals in every aspect of your life helps you immensely in managing expectations and leading a happy fulfilled life.

The next phase is to deal with mentality. Most people have formed a mentality of forming stereotypes on everyone they meet. For example, politicians are corrupt, men are cold-hearted, and women are opportunists and so on. The reality is quite different though; there are politicians who are honest in their work while there are men who are genuinely good. Generalization puts all fruit in one basket; be they good or bad and this generally affects your perception and attitude towards most people without even giving them a chance to justify themselves as worthy or innocent. The counselor as stated earlier will put emphasis on the importance of judging every situation in an independent manner and analyzing each aspect before drawing conclusions.

The therapy would transition into the solution thus you are advised to be genuine and true to yourself. You should not take the fall for what you are not guilty of which many people have a tendency of doing. This is a burden that they carry for a long time and it weighs heavily on them to the point of crushing them. Cognitive Behavioral Therapy assists you to let go and accept that some things are beyond your control. Accepting and understanding this will go a long way into bettering your life, behavior, attitude, and quality of decisions you make as pertaining to your life.

As the sessions draw to a conclusion the counselor will advise the patient to look at situations as they appear and work from there onwards rather than how according to them the situation should be in their favor and guilt themselves or those around them for that. Having this clarity will help you have some closure and understanding of where you stand and help you make the necessary steps into bettering your conditions rather than deceiving yourself and in the end, you finish at a worse position than you started.

Towards the concluding sessions, you will face your problems rather than ignoring them or running away. Many have tendencies of avoiding their bad situations thinking that everything will sort itself out if they wait it out. Unfortunately, that is far from the reality of the matter. The fact is the more you ignore the problem, the worse it may get. That is why it is imperative; you face your situations head-on. Deal with them and separate what you like from what you do not like. That is the basis of Cognitive Behavioral Therapy. That means how to analyze, and react to particular situations in your life; be they bad or good. Using rationale to reason and make conclusions instead of emotions which can be misleading. This can only be done if you are in control of your emotion and thoughts at all times.

The last phase of Cognitive Behavioral Therapy deals with evaluating, confirming and understanding yourself and those around you rather than drawing pre-assumed conclusions by yourself. We meet different people every day and therefore make so many assumptions or judgments upon people we do not even know that well. This is usually based on their appearances and first impressions. This according to Cognitive Behavioral Therapy is an erroneous way to approach situations and people. It is not only others but ourselves as well. People make judgments upon themselves drawing conclusions that they are weak and cannot handle certain situations without really even giving it a go. CBT, in this case, helps us get rid of negative thinking and form informed choices and decisions as per our lives and those in it. Understanding the situation and the person you are dealing with goes a long way in making your judgment and association with them worthwhile and your behavior or attitude towards them deserving or correct.

From these sessions or meetings, all that Cognitive Behavioral Therapy would result in the patient being able to make better choices and decisions towards his life without relying on emotions, as it can cloud your judgment. It is all about awareness of who you are, where you stand, what you stand for and how all other aspects of your life fit into all of this. Finding the right balance helps when you are making important decisions in life; your relationships for instance, your career, your job and your life in general. Partaking in Cognitive Behavioral Therapy would, in general, improve your quality of life and make you lead a stress-free and fulfilling life where you are aware and in control of everything and everyone in it.

How Then, Does a Patient Learn?

They can take place in the form of face to face meetings or as a group where you discuss what the patient learns and shares from his experiences and that of others and they can then gauge their progress as the discussions go further. The other way they learn is through frequent feedback. This allows them to gauge their own progress just as in the group discussions and also provides a platform to get opinions from an unbiased source which helps growth or recovery. The other way they learn is through the forms of body and mind-calming activities they are given they can then practice them and the more they do the better they get and the more fulfilled they become or feel.

The counselor can also advise the patient to put themselves out there more and experience the things they fear the most and this will be enough to strengthen reactions to hard situations. You can also keep or record your progress in a diary what this does is that it allows the patient review and assess themselves slowly with each day or week and look at which areas he or she needs to strengthen more or develop to accomplish his or her intended goals for the therapy. Cognitive Behavioral Therapy assists with insomnia, social fear or phobia, marital conflict, childhood issues, anger, panic disorders, and even drug and substance abuse and addiction.

The essence of this therapy is to help condition the thought process of individuals and help them make better decisions in their life when it comes to so many various aspects of life e.g. their finances, relationships, goals and overall attitude and behavior as a response to different stimuli both good and bad.

Cognitive Behavioral Therapy is quite advantageous. It is both time-saving and cost saving since it is a faster and effective therapy method in comparison to other therapies and also requires fewer therapy sessions which in turn relates to the spending of less money by the patients. This leads to the consumer getting better faster if he or she undertakes Cognitive Behavioral Therapy.

Cognitive Behavioral Therapy also leads to the diversification of provision since it's structured nature enables it to be provided in different formats such as in groups and in computer programs and thus it applies to a wide range of individuals. This, in turn, makes it a more sought method by most individuals who require therapy and which shows its effectiveness in comparison to other therapy forms.

Cognitive Behavioral Therapy also enhances the individual's rationality since it alters one thought to believe in logic and reason which in turn blocks negative thoughts and feelings from controlling the brain. Cognitive Behavioral Therapy, therefore, leads to improved brain performance which enhances the productivity of individuals who partake the therapy.

Cognitive Behavioral Therapy also focuses on an individual's control over their thoughts and belief systems thus enabling one to develop confidence in them in the long run. This, in turn, enables the patient to be able to tackle the everyday problems that they face in life which in turn minimizes over-dependence of the patient on other people or substances (drugs) so as to solve their problems.

Cognitive Behavioral Therapy places focus on altering the behavior of individuals which will result in making alterations of how a particular individual feels about themselves. This has a positive effect to the individual in the long run which ensures the patient is cured once and for all and thus saves the patient extra costs more therapy visits if the disorders were to be recurring.

Anxiety control is also learned when one takes Cognitive Behavioral Therapy since it gives the patient one clear guidelines on how to differently respond to anxiety as compared to their response in the past. Cognitive Behavioral Therapy thereby clearly enables the patient to learn how to handle situations in a more relaxing manner which in turn leads to effective decision making by the individual.

Cognitive Behavioral Therapy also engages the patient's mind during the therapy sessions which leaves no room for idleness in the mind of the patient which prevents situations such as addiction relapse (the recurrence of an unwanted past behavior occurring). Situations such as relapse are to be avoided at all costs since it leads to the stagnation of the patient's life, as they are dragged back to the unwanted behavior that limits their growth and prosperity.

Cognitive Behavioral Therapy is highly collaborative since the therapist works with the patient in finding the solution that the patient is currently facing, eliminates the aspect of rigidity that is experienced in the other forms of therapy as the therapist instructs the patient on what to do which mostly leads to negative results. Cognitive Behavioral Therapy, therefore, ensures that results are positive which ensures that the patient gets soon faster.

Cognitive Behavioral Therapy also implements the law of entropy and impermanence which means that it rests on the assumptions brought about by science which state that if you don't use it you will lose it. Cognitive Behavioral Therapy trains the human brain to create connections between frequent thoughts and emotions which assist individuals to constantly develop positive thinking, this leads to the prevention of disorder re-occurrence in the life of the patient.

Cognitive Behavioral Therapy is also highly pragmatic since it clearly identifies and outlines the specific problems that the patient faces and directs all the available resources into trying to solve those problems. This is important as it eliminates the vagueness of problem-solving which leads to unnecessary expenses that are easily avoidable. Since it is the most sought form of therapy it is thus clearly shown that Cognitive Behavioral Therapy tackles the necessary problems that the patients face.

Cognitive Behavioral Therapy gives the patient a more practical experience which is important in those concrete situations that the patient may face when he or she is alone. This practical experience is contextual and social in nature and it assists the patient in acquiring specific techniques that enable them to solve the problems that they face.

Emotional self-regulation of individuals which is the ability to respond to the demands with experience is also improved by Cognitive

Behavioral Therapy. This response is in such a manner that is socially tolerable and sufficiently flexible so as to permit and delay spontaneous reactions when and as needed. This, in turn, assists the patient to make critical decisions and within a short time period.

Cognitive Behavioral Therapy is also less demanding and flexible in comparison to other therapy forms since it can be conducted by oneself through a self-book or online. This is in contrast to other forms of therapy where the patient has to physically be present with the therapist so as to conduct a therapy session. This aspect of flexibility, therefore, encourages a lot of people to try out CBT to solve their problems.

Cognitive Behavioral Therapy aims in improving the comprehensive distancing behavior of individuals which is the ability of individuals to increase psychological flexibility. This refers to the ability of individuals to enter the present moment more fully in such a way that they can balance in either changing or persisting in indulging in a certain behavior as doing so serves their valued ends.

Cognitive Behavioral Therapy is a more tactical approach in problem-solving in comparison to other forms of therapy as it is conducted in a series of sessions with each session aimed at achieving specific goals, concepts, or techniques to work with. This enables the patient to practice specific techniques during the sessions that can be later applied in life when most needed.

Cognitive Behavioral Therapy also produces clear changes in thoughts and behavior that are easily measurable and thus it means that the patient can get quick results that he can measure and deduce whether he or she has improved from their current situation. This benefit has been proven since CBT has been extensively studied and the results from the studies have been constant and discrete.

Chapter 1: Relationship Factors When it Comes to CBT

The relationship between the patient and the therapist is one of the biggest elements when it comes to psychotherapy and has been discussed for a number of years. The relative significance has also been debated with some proponents claiming that it accounts for the majority of the changes though others say that a positive worrying alliance between the client and the therapist is necessary though it is not sufficient for change. Cognitive Behavioral Therapy has since received criticism for lack of attention to the relationship factors though this is a myth. Therapeutic relations are essential to collaboration and verifiability of improvement. The development of a strong relation needs empirically supported relationship elements like empathy, unconditional positive consideration,and respect towards the client. Understanding the internal reality of the client, showing concern and warmth for the welfare of the patient and developing something of a working alliance are all needed when it comes to cognitive behavioral therapies. The working alliance has been illustrated as therapist-to-client agreement on the therapeutic objectives and the tasks through which the objectives are going to be achieved and the formation of the bond between the patient and the specialist.

The Role of the Therapist

Source: https://www.goodtherapy.org/learn-about-therapy/types/cognitive-behavioral-therapy

The patients consider the therapists as experts in providing treatment and to behave in a professional way which means having professional boundaries and good interpersonal skills. Therapists that have a specialty in CBT need to balance several interpersonal demands when it comes to their role remaining particularly sensitive to what the patient wants and to the potential emotional reactions from the patient as well as, their reactions and thoughts concerning the client, session and therapy.

Expertise vs. Equality

When the treatment starts, the therapist is bound to present their expertise in a gracious manner and then describe their areas of experience and competence. This is as opposed to the myth CBT therapists are not likely to utilize the interpersonal processes like empathy in therapy and are probably going to come across as impersonal. Cognitive Behavioral Therapy generally tries to reduce the symptoms of the patient through cognitive or other behavior changes. As such, it focuses on the entire outcome as opposed to the process of the theory. The therapeutic process then exists in service of the clinically assessed outcome in CBT.

Interestingly, outcome literature has provided emphasis on technical or theory particular elements of treatment and sometimes relegated the significance of non-particular treatment factors. Research studies have tended to give emphasis on techniques like behavioral activation or cognitive restructuring as opposed to the relationship factors leading to changes in therapy. This emphasis has led to a strategy that encourages these particular non-specific factors to be controlled as opposed to studied in a direct manner. Some of the resultant myths as viewed in clinical practice and the theoretical literature is that the factors are the same across different therapy modes or that they are not as emphasized when it comes to Cognitive Behavioral Therapy which has created another myth that the therapeutic type alliance and other similar factors are not as important when it comes to CBT as compared to some of the other therapies.

One of the common assumptions is that CBT is presented in a technical way to the patient as opposed to a relationship with the patient. Basically, all Cognitive Behavioral Therapy texts provide great emphasis on the therapeutic relationship or the alliance in the outcome. These would include the original text as provided by Beck, A. and his colleagues that claimed the attributes including accurate empathy, warmth and being genuine are needed in order to come up with an optimum therapeutic effect. The other examples would pertain texts on relationships with patients that have more complicated issues.

Based according to an extensive review on the results as provided from the interpersonal behavior between the therapist and the client in Cognitive Behavioral Therapy, cognitive behavioral therapists tend to utilize relationship skills in the same way that therapists do from other theoretical orientations. Take for, there seems to be no particular difference in the frequency of therapist self-disclosure when it comes to insight-oriented therapy and Cognitive Behavioral Therapy and no link between outcome and self-disclosure.

The other thing is the therapeutic relations in CBT is attributed by a more active and directive stand on the part of therapists and higher levels of emotional support that would be seen in the insight-oriented therapies. Research done by Horvath in 2011 illustrated therapeutic alliance is reliably linked with outcome across different studies.Godfried and Eubanks Carter argued that self-disclosure is one of the most effective tools when it comes to strengthening the facilitating change and alliance in Cognitive Behavioral Therapy. There seems to be no particular difference in the frequency of therapist self-disclosure between cognitive behavioral and insight-oriented therapy. Contrary to a number of myths there does not seem to be a lot of strong information which shows cognitive-behavioral specialists are technical and otherwise cold in the manner that they operate.

If a client asks the therapist a question concerning a treatment matter, the best thing to do would be to answer it to the best of one's abilities. If you do not know the answer and it would be something that relates to the client's disorder or treatment then it is fine to say so and access the information and bring it to the next session.Similarly, having an area of expertise may not mean that you are an expert when it comes to the client. The client may also have different areas of expertise which is not related to treatment which is admitted would lead to a relationship of experts that have different skills sets working to solve different problems. That relationship would then lead to collaboration that is set as the active engagement of the client within the shared work of therapy. The relations between the cognitive behavioral therapist and the client are not one that is of complete equality as the client is consulting the therapist as an expert and professional.

The therapist needs to know that several of the clients will see them as powerful especially when they feel vulnerable. This is played out in several means such as the way the client addresses the therapist such as the setting of the sessions and the payment arrangements for work. As an expert, the therapist also becomes an educator. When information is given to the therapist's clients the qualities of a good teacher then become significant. These qualities include being clear and gearing what is being said. You do not have to talk down to the client or use language which the client would not understand. Some of the clients would perceive the provision of scientific articles as a sign of respect while others would just be overwhelmed by the material. The therapist needs to remain sensitive as depending on the level of understanding of the client, not to mention their needs and interests.

A patient that has a post-graduate degree, for example, would need a different psycho-educational set of materials as compared an individual that did not finish high school. The therapist should not make any assumption concerning the resources which are available to the customer and should not hesitate in asking any questions

Coping as Opposed to Mastery

The therapist is often the model for the clients either in an implicit or explicit manner. For example, it would be common to utilize the role-playing and other modeling exercises during sessions. Though one is not expected to be an expert in these areas especially when practicing communication or other particular skills as a matter of fact, it may not be helpful for an individual to seem to be the perfect person to the clients as it can put them off or intimidate them from their attempts at opening up about themselves considering they would already see you as an accomplished person and very knowledgeable. As such, the patients often learn more with the use of a coping model, than they would from the masterysetting. It is a bit reassuring for the clients when they see the therapist make mistakes and acknowledge them then move on to the improvement of their behavior because it tells them that they can also follow on the same path toward wellness. Therapists are,after all, human beings and it can give hope to the clients to know this fact. It can also be useful at times to make mistakes on purpose during the practice exercises such that the patients have a chance so they can give their suggestions. If the patient provides feedback on the performance during a session then that is a sign they are comfortable doing it and it is crucial that the therapist does not take offense or become defensive. The ability for an individual to learn from their mistakes, and then enact change, and take on different perspectives is part of the growth model for the patient. At the same time when the therapist provides feedback or suggestions, they would be framed in the manner of an opinion rather than a statement of fact. The specialist also needs to encourage the patients in order to attain opinions from other individuals that they would respect.

The Utilization of Self-Disclosure

Self-disclosure may be effective as a tool when it comes to Cognitive Behavioral Therapy. It includes different modes of communication which can be set according to the disclosure of content as opposed to process. The content disclosure would also mean the manner that you respond to questions which are asked by the client. One of the useful guidelines when it comes to self-disclosure is not answering the question that you do not feel comfortable with by stating the fact. The recommendation is that the therapist does not follow the statement with another which would hint the client was wrong to ask or which turns the question back towards the patient.

You should also consider the intentions of the client that has asked the question in order to establish credibility or experience or just to make conversation so as to be polite. It is the responsibility of the therapist to answer the queries clearly concerning the background, training,and experience. The patients are naturally curious concerning the therapist and sharing some information on their life can assist the patient to view them as human. It is impossible not to share information sometimes. The patients are likely to notice the décor when they come to the office or the books which are on the shelf. A number of clients may even do an online search concerning the therapist prior to the appointment in order to see their resume and past experience. That way when they come for the session they will already have formed various opinions concerning ability. The therapist could choose to occasionally disclose the problems which they have come across and the way they have been dealt with. One of the guidelines for this self-disclosure is it would be for the sake of treatment and has the interests of the patient at the core. If there is a personal problem which is disclosed then it would be the one that has already been solved and it is not something which would lead the client to be concerned as concerns wellbeing.

The therapist needs to consider the purpose of disclosure very carefully. They should then think about it if it if it is going to normalize the concerns of the patient and whether it would assist the patient to see the therapist as a person that has their own problems and uses Cognitive Behavioral Therapy in order to solve them. Are the strategies that the therapist using for himself some of the same they are proposing for treatment?

Process-oriented self-disclosure includes the therapist sharing their emotional response types and automatic thoughts had with the patient, especially if they happen to have interpersonal issues. This disclosure mode would be invaluable to the patients as a number of people do not usually get honest feedback from those who are in their lives. If a client seems angry or aggressive, then they may have interpersonal rejection from other individuals without explanation. It would be very helpful to these patients to give feedback including the responses of the therapist during the session. At the same time, the disclosure that the patient has become sad or worried in response to the client may be useful in itself.

If the therapist shares his reactions then it would be significant to frame them as an example of the reaction as opposed to the definitive or the only response that the client would get. As such, the therapist would need to be sure to take personal responsibility for their own actions. He or she cannot speak for the way people could react to the client.

Meta-Cognition

Source:
https://www.kidscooperate.com/blog/cognitive-behavioral-therapy-autism

In order to use self-disclosure concerning the therapeutic relations, the therapist has to be aware at the metacognitive level and utilize this information in the session. This process is to be aware concerning the needs of the patient concerning the content of what they are saying, the emotional reactions they may have toward the situation and attention to particular strategies utilized during the session. It also concerns being aware concerning the different nuances of the reaction of the client such as not only what they may say but what their body language and facial expressions communicate. The observation of the individual would then be posted as the hypotheses so that the client can agree or choose not to within the comments. This skill would require the therapist's ability to listen and observe the client and themselves.

Chapter2: Problems Faced by Individuals Who Seek Help in Cognitive Behavioral Therapy

The individuals that seek assistance from Cognitive Behavioral Therapy usually experience the following problems: Chronic pain which is a condition influenced by psychological, biological, and social factors. Cognitive Behavioral Therapy aims to manage the biological causes and also its psychological and social influences and consequences. CBT achieves this since it focuses on small and statistically significant benefits for disability.

Post-Traumatic Stress Disorder (PTSD) is also another problem faced by those that seek assistance from Cognitive Behavioral Therapy. PTSD is a disorder that is associated with the failure to recover after experiencing a terrifying event. CBT encourages patients suffering from PTSD to reevaluate their thinking patterns and assumptions so as to identify unhelpful patterns (distortions) in thoughts which assist them in developing positive thoughts.

Patients suffering from Bipolar disorders also seek assistance from CBT. Bipolar disorder is a disorder that is associated with extreme mood swings ranging from depressive lows to manic highs. CBT assists the patient in monitoring the occurrence, severity, and course of the manic-depressive symptoms which will enable the patients to overcome this disorder.

Obsessive Compulsive Disorder (OCD) patients also seek assistance from Cognitive Behavioral Therapy. OCD is associated with those individuals who have excessive thoughts (obsessions) which lead to repetitive behaviors (compulsions). CBT treats OCD through exposure and response prevention where the therapist assists the patient to create a detailed list of his or her symptoms. During the therapy sessions, the patient is exposed to their fears drafted in the list in a chronological order, and with the therapist's guidance, the patient is guided on how to overcome these fears.

Patients suffering from specific phobia which is an anxiety disorder that amounts to unreasonable fear of the exposure to specific objects or situations also seek assistance from Cognitive Behavioral Therapy. CBT exposes the patient to his or her fear which in turn leads to less anxiety from the patient towards the fears by enabling the patient to gain control over their associated phobia.

Cognitive Behavioral Therapy also assists patients with problems of low esteem that makes them feel bad about themselves more than they are confident in themselves. Cognitive Behavioral Therapy assists these patients in altering their functional patterns that are dysfunctional and also b changing their behavior patterns which makes them feels stuck. This, in turn, improves the patient's confidence in the long run.

Work-Related Stress (WRS) is also another problem that is faced by those individuals that seek CBT assistance. WRS is stress that mainly arises for work-related areas or situations since the patient perceives the work environment in such a manner that makes him or her not to cope effectively at the workplace. CBT changes the way of thinking of a patient by giving them tips on learning to problem solve or to get rid of self-defeating thoughts which usually leads to their demotivation. This will, in turn, improve the patient's ability to experience less stress in the workplace.

Patients suffering from depression (a disorder characterized by a persistently depressing mood and a loss of interest in activities which eventually causes a significant impairment in daily life activities of an individual's life) also seek assistance from CBT. Depression is tackled by Cognitive Behavioral Therapy as the therapist assists the patient to identify situations in the life of the patient that may be leading to their depression. The distorted perceptions and current thinking patterns are identified and then tackled which in turn minimizes the depression of the individual in the long run.

Those people who suffer from negative automatic thinking also seek assistance from Cognitive Behavioral Therapy. Negative automatic thinking is as a disorderwhereby an individual has automatic thoughts especially negative ones which mostly arise from the negative beliefs that people hold about themselves which in turn negatively affect their lives. CBT provides clear guidelines to the individuals on how they will focus their energy on positive thinking which in turn will lead to the lives being improved.

Somatoform disorders are also another problem faced by those individuals who seek assistance from CBT. This is a disorder that is associated with a mental disorder which its symptoms are shown physically in the form of illness or injury but the disorder cannot be easily be detected by a medical examiner who cannot also fully explain the condition. Cognitive Behavioral Therapy focuses on a way of calming down the mind from outlaying any form of disturbance that can be physically projected.

Patients with Chronic Fatigue Syndrome (CFS) a disease that is associated with profound fatigue, sleep abnormalities, and pain also seek assistance from therapy that's associated with CBT. It has been proven that this form of therapy is able to greatly assist them. CBT achieves by alleviating the exercise fears of the patient which will reverse the deconditioning that usually accompanies the illness which will in turn counter the Chronic Fatigue Syndrome.

Cognitive Behavioral Therapy is also critical in assisting ladies who have pregnancy complications and female hormonal conditions whereby they have abnormal hormone secretions mainly caused by anxiety and the food ingested which leads to them having a lot of difficulties during childbirth. Cognitive Behavioral Therapy teaches the lady how to identify and deal with the situations that can trigger the feelings of anxiety. This will, in turn, enable the lady to handle her feelings without the aid of drugs.

Eating disorders are also another problem that can be managed by Cognitive Behavioral Therapy since it assists the patient in the reduction of impulse control which reduces the urge of binge eating. CBT also assists patients to become more self-controlling around 'Trigger Foods' which will lead them to minimize their food consumption.

Anger and aggression issues are also dealt with Cognitive Behavioral Therapy as it uses certain components and techniques with one of the techniques referred to as the ABC model. A stand for Activating Events which refers to anything either imagined or real that activates our belief systems and influences our reaction. B stands for beliefs which are influenced by the activating events, which lead to an emotional consequence. C which stands for consequence sets the stage of what will follow after one engages in certain rash actions. By using these components of CBT model one is taught on the procedure of anger management.

Cognitive Behavioral Therapy also aims at treating personality disorders which is a type of mental disorder associated with the patient having trouble in relating to people and situations due to their rigid and unhealthy thinking patterns. Cognitive Behavioral

Therapy through the use of constant interactive techniques between the therapist and the patient enables the patient to learn how to associate with other individuals which will, in turn, improve their relationships with people.

Disadvantages of Cognitive Behavioral Therapy

Although Cognitive Behavioral Therapy has a lot of advantages it also has some disadvantages which comprise of the following: Due to its structured nature CBT is not applicable to individuals who have more complex mental health needs or complex learning activities since it mainly involves talking sessions with therapists and thus cannot deal with complex problems such as insanity which require medical attention.

Cognitive Behavioral Therapy is also solely focused on dealing with the problems that face the individual such as their behavior, thoughts, and feelings. It does not address the bigger problems that face society and in families which often have a significant impact on an individual's health and wellbeing.

Cognitive Behavioral Therapy also enhances a sense of discomfort to the patients since they have to share some of their anxieties and emotions with the therapist. Some of those emotions are deemed private by the patient and thus he or she will have a difficult time sharing them with another individual in the form of a therapist.

Cognitive Behavioral Therapy focuses on positive self-evaluations which may at times be maladaptive and dysfunctional since in most occasions it is the positive rather than the negative self-assessment that is characterized by aspects of bias and inaccuracies in fields such as health and education.

Cognitive Behavioral Therapy also confuses the symptoms of depression with the cognitive causes of depression. This, in turn, leads to the patient being misguided by the advice he or she receives from the therapist and which in turn lead to persistence of the disorders that the patient is suffering from. Thus CBT is not a very good method for solving disorders such as depression.

Chapter3: How CBT Works in a Holistic Manner

Source:https://www.greenhousetreatment.com/therapy/holistic-therapy/

Cognitive behavior therapy appeals to those who are in the medical profession as the method makes sense from an intuitive perspective which is easy to comprehend and is consistent considering the medical model. Those patients issued with homework and education which is not unlike what the doctors do tell individuals about the disease and have the expectations of them being compliant. Patients experience illness rather than the disease. Illness means that the symptoms alter the relationships, the potential for future planning and the sense of self. What illness means to the patient would be affected deeply through the way dependence is tolerated and if the care is given throughout the life of the patient. The meaning of experience is what the psychodynamic therapists consider. These therapists are concerned with the reduction of the symptoms and they address the manner that the patients assess symptoms and problems. Though the treatment effectiveness for psychodynamic therapy is broad and steep in its scope and that could be part of the reason why it has been found to be longer.

As such, holistic holds that the consciousness is not housed in any part of the individual though it is an integration of the mind, body and the spirit. Those who practice holistic approaches for CBT believe in the view of each person as the whole being which is essential in giving care and typically collaborate the ones in therapy to assist them in gaining awareness of the connections between the thoughts emotions and physical experiences. The therapy can assist individuals to get to know that each component works together in harmony so as to support daily functions. This understanding for the self may usually lend itself to a better awareness and self-acceptance. Holistic therapy does not work in order to eliminate the symptoms though. This is an approach that views the symptoms as one means the consciousness of the individual would bring attention to the higher level of awareness for the person.

To develop a sense of awareness through the means of holistic therapy, the practitioners have to work less in order to assist the people have changed and more to keep them thinking about the present moment. At the time this acceptance is achieved then the individuals would have the chance to let go of their resistance and that would allow relaxation and release of fears.

CBT via holistic therapy considers intervention on different levels which are the body, mind, and the emotions. The original exercises in holistic therapy consider such things as massage and bodywork which focuses the attention of the individual on different areas of tension within the body. These are believed to be the places where there are manifestations of emotions which have been repressed. Once the trust is attained between the therapist and the patient, then the therapist would assist the person to relieve their bodily tension. This then allows the individual to become better receptive to a number of emotions they were not capable of perceiving earlier. The next exercise would be the utilization of different verbal forms of psychotherapy in the process of understanding the emotions coming from the release of body tension. Both patient and therapist explore the emotions and the role played within the life of the individual. At times, the therapist can emphasize the repression of the patient concerning these motions. Although, only at the time the decision to repress the different emotions has been realized can the holistic sessions proceed.

Value of Cognitive Behavioral Therapy

When it comes to cognitive behavior therapy, the goal of the specialist is to focus on the objectives as depending on the needs provided by the patient. In any treatment including CBT the changing modes of thought emotional reactions or habitual behavior, it is not easy if the patients do not have the required motivation. It is also demotivating for the patients in the event that the goals of the therapy are far from the reality that they are not able to visualize the number of steps in order to realize them. At the same time, the changes which achieved during the course of therapy are transient if they are not consistent with the life values of the patient. At the same time, it is the assessment of the life values of the patient and the connecting of the therapy goals with their satisfaction which is one of the important sources of motivation for parents.

Some forms of psychotherapy concern looking to the history of the patient in order to gain understand of the current feelings. On the other hand, Cognitive Behavioral Therapy will consider the present thought about a situation. It may also assist individuals with a number of problems where the beliefs and thoughts are significant. It focuses on the need to identify and change the manner in which the individual sees a situation. In CBT the pattern of thinking of a person can be likened to wearing a pair of glasses which makes people see the world in a particular way. The theory makes people more aware of how the thought patterns create our reality and determine the way that people behave.

Changing Perceptions and Distortions

Cognitive behavior therapy has the objective of transforming the ways of thinking and behaving which stand in the way of the positive outcome. If a person has depression, for example, their interpretations and perceptions of reality are very much distorted.

This distortion of the way they see things can lead to jumping to conclusions or seeing things as worse than they actually are, thereby blowing things out of proportion. If people learn fearful or negative thought patterns then they can start thinking in this manner automatically. Cognitive behavior theory would focus on challenging of these automatic thoughts and then comparing them with reality. If a person may alter their thought process, then the distress would decrease and so they would function in a manner which is likely to benefit them and the people that are around them.

When it comes to depression treatment, cognitive behavior therapy is one of the best known and empirically supported treatments for depression. CBT is believed to work so well when relieving the symptoms of depression as it produces changes in cognition which fuel cycles of negative feelings and rumination. According to the Cognitive Behavioral Therapy for Mood Disordersjournal,Cognitive Behavioral Therapy is so protective against those episodes of acute depression, that it can be used in place of the anti-depressant medications.

It has also shown a lot of promise as an approach for assisting with the handling of postpartum depression and as an adjunct to the medical treatment when it comes to bipolar patients. Similarly, preventive cognitive therapies as paired with antidepressants have been found to assist the patients that experienced reoccurring depression. It may also interfere with maintenance for unhealthy body weights, reduce feelings of isolation and assist patients to get more comfortable around trigger foods situations which are exposure therapy.

The Stages of Cognitive Behavioral Therapy

There are four significant phases to CBT treatment where you and your therapist work together at each of the stages. The first one is the assessment stage. This phase which is also known as the forming of an alliance entails you and the therapist getting to know each other. The therapist is the one that comes up with a treatment plan and often has an idea concerning how long the treatment is going to take. When you have the first session, you should have the expectation of spending time with the practitioner and get to know each other. The therapist is like going to provide an explanation on the way that the entire process of CBT works. Different therapists have their own renditions so do not expect that it is going to be the same as illustrated in this text.

The therapist is then likely to ask queries about your state. This is so that he or she is able to make an evaluation concerning the treatment method which would be adequate for your case. You also need to be specific concerning that which affects you the most. The therapist might ask what you hope to gain from therapy. It would be helpful if it were possible to explain how you would like your life to be after successful therapy.

What to Expect

By the end of the first session, you should have a strong feeling the therapist is looking out for your interests. You need to feel positive concerning working together with the therapist in order to make things in your life that much better. In the jargon of CBT that would be to say working together in this manner is also known as a therapeutic alliance and is significant when it comes to cognitive behavioral theories.

If you do not have this strong feeling then you need to consider whether the therapist is the right fit. You need to be sure to mention this at the start of the second session. The CBT therapy may not be successful if you do not form an alliance at the beginning. By the end of the first session or the second one, the therapist may have a treatment plan in their mind. This may enable the therapist to come up with an estimation of the number of sessions required for the purpose of treatment. There is no fixed pattern when it comes to CBT treatment. The plan could change though considering you would move unexpectedly quickly. It may also change because something may come about and there would need to be extra time in order to address.

Understanding Your Thoughts

This is the cognitive part of Cognitive Behavioral Therapy, where one learns to understand and control their thought process. You and the therapist work would have to work together so as to understand your thought process. You may spend a bit of time discussing things which happened in the past that had something to do with the manner that you developed as an individual. At times the way that a person thinks is the result of how you learned to process things during your past. In this phase of the CBT, the specialist would spend time with you getting to know the particular contexts of your past. In the CBT terminology, the thought processes in your past which influence your thinking at the present would be called schemas. At times, you may consider different things in a particular manner as it seems to be the only reasonable path of action. Your therapist may also explore whether the ways you think about things are also reasonable. As such, they will discuss the evidence with you. On the other hand, you may also decide to try some experiments in order to get to the most reasonable way of processing situations. In between the therapy sessions, you may also perform different activities which are connected to this work. You may try to keep the records of your thoughts for each day.

Stage 2 is not particularly clear cut though as one is not able to tell with ease when it starts and when it comes to a close. There is time spent understanding thought processes in each of the therapy sessions. By the time that you have had different CBT sessions, you would begin to understand your thought process. This would allow you to see the way your thought process is related to the particular symptoms being addressed. You would also start to find ways of controlling your thoughts such that you can consider your symptoms.

Behavior Stage

The third is the behavior stage where you and the specialist selected will work on the adoption of new and healthy patterns of thought. You will then apply these new patterns of thought and act differently. When it comes to the behavioral part of CBT, you begin to understand the way that your thoughts and your and behavior influence one another. Sometimes the things you do influence your thought process. Your thought process also affects your behavior. During this stage of therapy, you start to establish particular patterns of thought and action which would assist in the management of your problems. Between the therapy sessions, you can do activities which are related to these patterns. In an example, you may practice interactions with people in different ways. You may also practice the handling of different scenarios and in so doing gain control over what is happening.

This third stage is not especially clear cut as one is not able to easily tell when it ends and the time that it begins. You may spend a bit of time working on different behavior depending on the therapy sessions that you take part in. though by the time that one approaches the end of the cognitive behavior treatment; you need to be applying what you have learned in real life situations between the sessions.

Learning Stage

At this time you and the therapist work so that they can make sure the changes stick. At this time you will learn to utilize the principles of CBT for yourself going forward in order for you to cope with events in the future without the need for further therapy. Towards the end of the CBT treatment, one may become prepared to complete the process of therapy and deal with symptoms solely. In a sense, the therapy process may not stop entirely. The sessions with the therapist are the ones which are going to stop though you can continue the treatment alone. You become the therapist for yourself which sounds quite risky. One of the significant differences between CBT and the other treatments is when it comes to CBT you get to know how to deal with your condition. In the event that you have a long-term condition, the advantages of the CBT will proceed in the long term. If your condition is addressed by CBT therapy, then you can still use these methods by yourself in the future.

In the same way as other CBT stages, the learning process may not have clearly defined boundaries. You may start to work on your own symptoms in the early parts of the CBT treatment though. As you approach the end of the treatment, you need to have great confidence so you are able to practice those things that you have come to learn by yourself. Cognitive behavior therapy has to allow you to become independent and to manage your condition without having the therapist intervene. The four stages of CBT are not always in separate as they can become a bit mixed. This is because cognitive behavior theory is not rigid as a system that has fixed regulations.

Chapter 4: Intrusive Thoughts and How to Deal with Them

For some time psychologists have known that every normal person experiences all kinds of impulses and thoughts including those which are perverse, dark, or violent. These are referred to as challenging automatic or intrusive thought which pops into the minds of people without their control. In the late 70s, psychologists that were studying obsessive thought asked a group of normal individuals whether they had experienced intrusive thoughts in their life and the composition of these thoughts. There was a discovery soon after the majority of the test group admitted they had experienced this phenomenon. The interesting aspect of the nature of the thoughts was they alluded to several things such as thoughts of violence, harming, crashing their car while driving, harming and killing people or even jumping in front of a speeding vehicle.

Two years later a different group of psychologists produced a paper which described the development of a survey known as the Automatic Thoughts Questionnaire. Researchers provided a big group of the students with a list of the thoughts which could have popped into their minds during the week which passed. The psychologists again found that the volunteers, in this case, were experiencing negative thoughts at random intervals which degraded themselves.

The question is whether having negative thoughts affects the state of mental health. The research which has been done on the subject tends to find a relationship between the frequency of these types of thoughts with things like anxiety and sadness. As such, it is true that having more negative thoughts are then linked to negative feelings. On the other hand, the link between them is not straightforward. Both clinical research and the practice which has been done illustrates that having these thoughts solely does not cause any harm. After all, they can be found in people that are said to be healthy and well-functioning. The question then transforms to what separates the healthy from the unhealthy when it comes to intrusive thoughts. Whether the intrusive thought causes problems is dependent on the manner that you respond to it. Ask yourself if you believe having the thought is a sign of something. Also, consider if you try to control these thoughts or do something in order to prevent them from coming true. Does it potentially mean that you are a bad individual?

If the answer is yes to the first two questions then you are more likely to suffer both psychological and negative effects. It is not just the occurrence of the thoughts within your psyche which causes pathology rather it is the way that you react to them. When individuals start to take these thoughts a bit too seriously and assume that there is truth in them, then the depression and the OCD may start to increase. The fact is that Cognitive Behavioral Therapy usually entails the assisting of patients so they can learn that these intrusive thoughts are either harmless or not indicative of their underlying natures. Research studies based on the patients that make the biggest improvements in therapy entail the ones that learn to see their thoughts through a different spectrum which is not negative.

Negative automatic thoughts, otherwise referred to as NATs if taken seriously or obsessed on can lead to anxiety, irritability, depression, and self-doubt. They are not particularly helpful or useful though everyone has them. The difference concerning whether people believe them or accept them or challenge them is influential on how mentally happy and healthy your life is going to be.

How to Identify the Negative Automatic Thoughts

They are always negative; statements like you are useless because you got into an accident on the road, failed an exam, or did not get a call back on an interview are part of the overreactions that you may have which come from these negative automatic thoughts.

They make you see yourself in a negative light: these thoughts are always very self-critical towards you as an individual and make you see yourself as less than worthy to exist within your space. They make you feel bad about your life in general.

They are self-sabotaging: they make you self-doubt or aid in self-destructive behaviors such as encouraging you to end a healthy relationship which has been ongoing because the thought is it will end anyway. You may even convince yourself to quit your job because the thoughts claim that you are no good and will get fired anyway.

They are uninvited: in the same way as the rude gate crasher who thinks you need to be told how bad the party is, they are intensely critical. They appear at times when you did not think they would come and sometimes ruin a good mood even when you are having a high.

They may be believable but they are biased: it can be plausible to think in a negative manner about you. This is especially when you make a small mistake such as dropping a plate or being clumsy. The thought may come in as an overreaction and not an objective assessment of what has happened. It will sound something like 'that is why you cannot have anything nice, you break everything.' They seem to be acceptable but they are wrong. Just because you may have done performed well at one thing does not mean that you are never going to do well at anything.

How to Cope with Unwanted Thoughts

Psychologists usually make the distinctions between the automatic and controlled thoughts in this manner. They are usually triggered by things which are in our environments even though at times they are completely random. For example, you may be thinking about something and a song just pops into your head at random and not in line with what you were thinking about. A mistake that is made most of the time is to obsess and to assign some meaning to the automatic and intrusive thoughts. They are of the belief that this has to say something about who they are as people or they assume that the thought holds some truth especially if the thought happens to be self-critical. When you take the thoughts at face value then it can land you in a lot of trouble. Some therapists use the analogy of a mailbox. At any time in the day, anyone can decide to drop notes or letters into the mailbox. In the same way, a lot of people cannot prevent the brain from sending these intrusive thoughts into their consciousness. If you went into the mailbox and saw a note which claimed that you were a terrible person or you were a violent individual, then you would not just take the note to be correct and start thinking that you are indeed a bad person. You are also not able to control your thoughts but you do have some form of control concerning your response to these thoughts. Obviously, this is not always the easy thing to do as it may at times need the assistance of a specialist.

Cognitive Behavioral Techniques for Intrusive Thoughts

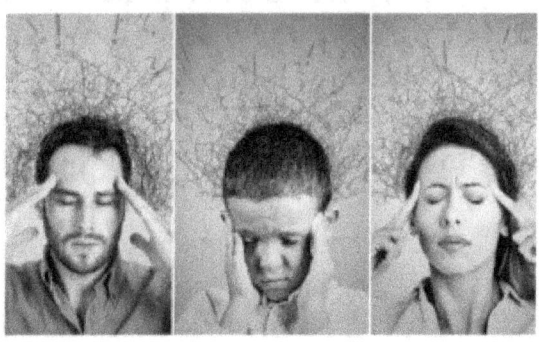

Source: https://cbtpsychologicalassociates.com/ocd-and-intrusive-thoughts/

Having negative, obsessive ideas is a big source of suffering. It would be one thing which could intensify the cycle of anxiety in so doing. It may even dig you deeper into your hole as you surround yourself with impulses and images which are not helpful whatsoever. During these times hearing the words to calm down and stop worrying about things which have not occurred yet is the least bit helpful. Whether you like it or not, the mind is an endless factory of ideas. The unfortunate thing is what it produces may not always be the most helpful when it comes to the achievement of goals or even feeling better about yourself as a person. Everyone has unhelpful and absurd ideas though under the normal conditions you may not give the reasoning too much power. Instead, you may want to prioritize the encouragement of helpful thoughts. When you go through periods of stress, or anxiety, the intrusive thoughts become more and more frequent. You may also give these thoughts more power than they would deserve. The following are some cognitive behavioral techniques which would be effective during times like these.

Scheduling Positive Activities

Schedule rewarding activities during the course of the day, in terms of setting quality time for yourself tends to come up with positive results. These activities tend to be simple such as going out for a movie whose release, you have been waiting for. You may also give yourself a few days break from work by asking for leave or buy a book and make a good meal for yourself and your loved ones.

Hierarchy of Concerns

Intrusive thoughts tend to resemble smoke from a chimney as it is the heat of something which is smoldering inside. This fire consists your unresolved issues and gets worse over the course of time. The first step, in this case, would be controlling the focus on your feelings and thoughts and the frustration would be to clarify them. This is done by making a hierarchy of problems. The scale of the concerns goes from low to high. You can begin by noting everything which bothers you. You need to be visualizing the rate of the chaos within you in the same manner as a brainstorm.

The next thing would be to make a hierarchy beginning with the things that you consider to be small problems and ending in the ones which you feel are too overwhelming. Once the visual order has been set then you need to reflect on each of the points. At this time, you can think rationally and then arrive at solutions for each of them.

Thought Records

These allow us to apply logic to the way that we process things. Think of an individual that is afraid of losing their job. Overnight, they would be obsessed with the fact management thinks they are doing everything in the wrong way. This cycle could result in a self-fulfilling process. Through thinking about everything which can go wrong, sooner or later he is going to end up doing something very wrong. The reason is he has fallen into a negative state of mind which self-sabotages and subconsciously fulfills the commands of his negative willpower. In order to have a better sense of balance, control, and coherence, there is nothing which helps more than making a record of the invasive thoughts that you have and their frequency. You may then decide to consider the level of truth for these negative thoughts.

The people who have OCD may be seen as phobic if you do not do a ritual. If it is possible to assist them to relax by washing their hands not hundreds of times but only once, then you can assist them to relax with moving away from the prop of the ritual. Once you assuage the anxiety, you can look at assisting the clients to gain a better sense of better control within their lives. It is at that point during the treatment that you can start to address the thoughts and behaviors.

CBT Technique for OCD: Finding the Underlying Need

Once you have taught the client to relax, you can consider which extent the OCD has been sloppy at meeting their main emotional needs and teach the client what it means. From there the specialist can rehearse mentally a typical time in which the OCD emerges with the use of the SALT technique: in this case, SALT would entail the following:

- Stopping and concentrating of that which is happening at the time.
- Enquiring from the OCD what it would want to do for you at the moment.
- Listening to what it wants to do for you like trying to make you feel safe or in control.
- Think of means that you are going to feel safer or more in control of the OCD and then note these down.

For example, if you had taught the client breathing techniques for the sake of fast relaxation or even self-hypnosis, these are some of the ways that they would be able to relax. In order to relax, you would have to feel safe. It is possible to look at the way they can meet these basic needs in healthier means.

CBT technique for OCD: Focusing On and Trusting the Observable Reality

Considering OCD motivates individuals that tend to mismanage their imagination and then discriminate fantasy over the observable reality it would be useful to assist people to focus on the present. One exercise which is sometimes shared with people experiencing OCD would be to have them close their eyes and have them do an exercise in perception. Tell them you are going to snap your fingers and have them tell you when you clapped and when they had imagined that you clapped. You have never had anyone be unable to distinguish the real from the imagined sounds. That builds the confidence of the clients in trusting the senses over what is imagined.

The next step would be to relax and envisage a lot of the times that the OCD tried to make it seem likeyou not trust your actions and they may find that they trust their perspective to know that door is locked or their hands are clean so they do not have to do it all over again. The specialist may also ask them to focus on those things which they are able to see such as windows, floors, and other people. They will then run through their mind things concerning the door, things concerning the window, and so forth. This would also be referred to as a distraction technique but it is also one of the ways of going from imagination towards observation. The calmer that the person is able to rehearse performing this within their mind, the easier it is going to be when the OCD comes and tries it on their psyche.

Externalizing the OCD

It may be a cliché to claim that a person is not the embodiment of the OCD. That is not to say that the problem is not important. The objective is to have the clients use this knowledge in order that they beat the overall problem. This would be opposed to labeling an individual. It is also a way of peeling off the label, as such.

As a thought experiment, it is possible to assist the patient to personify and so externalize the OCD. In this case, the following would come into view:

- The arguments it utilizes in order to convince one and waste their time
- The persuasion techniques that are utilized
- What it promises the individual
- The lies that it tells about an individual

Removing the condition from the core person of the individual is a key skill that every CBT practitioner aspires towards. This is also the way that a specialist would treat a chronic smoker and other people that are matted to addictions.

The Stop Technique

Consider if you have repetitive negative thoughts swirling in your psyche that you would want to be rid of. You may be having irrational feelings of anger, paranoia, and jealousy or perhaps you experience negative self-criticism which undermines your level of confidence. The stop technique is something that you can do yourself though there are some who might need professional assistance in this approach. For example, if you are assisting your child then explain that the two of you are going to embark on something to assist with the alleviation of their negative thoughts.

You may have a shot of doing it yourself as well by following a number of steps.

1. Stay 'Stop!' when you start to experience a recurring negative thought. This may be done aloud or it can just be to yourself.
2. Negate the thought but do it in a positive way through the exchange of the negative thought for a positive. Replace statements such as you cannot

or will not with you are able to do something.
3. Take a breath or even learn useful breathing techniques in order to assist with relaxing as opposed to feeling anxious and say the peaceful thoughts out loud or within your mind at a repeated rate up to the point that the negative, intrusive thoughts go away.
4. Complete these steps every instance that you notice the occurrence of an intrusive thought

Stress Inoculation Approaches

Stress inoculation training otherwise referred to as SIT along with cognitive behavior therapy is very good at the prevention of developing a chronic post-traumatic stress disorder. This approach also increases the rate of recovery for the female victims of sexual violence that had PTSD according to the department of health and human services. This Stop method is part of the coping skills that are given during the SIT procedures. Some of the other coping skills include deep muscle relaxation training, role-playing, positive thinking, and breathing exercises

Most patients are able to adjust to their lives after serious conditions like cancer and subsequent treatment. Though there are others that do not and come up with adjustment disorders, such as agoraphobia or other phobias related to their social engagements. A patient that is having problems adjusting back into their social settings would experience anxiety and other problems which are much more severe than expected and cause issues for them within their home or working environment. This Stop approach is just one component of a treatment plan which would assist with the improvement of life for the patients that have issues adjusting into their lives after being treated for cancer. The adjusting problems experienced during and after cancer treatment may be complex as mental problems which have to get professional assistance for the treatment to be successful.

CBT and Spirituality

In the same way as all therapists, CBT specialists work with religious clients. Considering that cognitively oriented specialists would identify and challenge the beliefs of the client. There is a risk that the deeply held beliefs of the patient as pertaining to their religious background could be shaken. At the same time, because it is practiced as a radical modernist type of scientific paradigm, CBT has faced a lot of criticism for overlooking things such as evil, grace, and transcendence.

Is Spirituality Relevant When It Comes to CBT

For millennia people have considered faith and religious belief to be the answer to their emotional and mental problem. The bulk of the research done up to the present illustrates that having a belief in something is overall great for your mental health problems. Religions have created charities which were there to particularly assist mental health issues. As such, CBT was created from the empirical studies which did not consider initially faith as a particular variable. Though as investigations concerning the role of religious belief and practice continued to grow in their popularity, evidence accumulated in particular groups for random and controlled trials of Cognitive Behavioral Therapy adapted for Judaism and Christianity. There are researchers who have come up with models on the means to include it within the CBT creations such as

Hebblethwaite and Williams, though they had not been the subject of the trials. A lot of this particular research has been done by people from a religious background in areas of high adherence to faith such as the southern united states, on the other hand the picture within places such as the United Kingdom is that of a range of beliefs among the therapists and clients with different attitudes concerning how relevant the interaction between faith and health.

Religious Models Concerning the Mind

The major religions in the world have models of the human psyche and a consideration of the way that the mind and the spirit interact with each other. It is not feasible to provide an exhaustive list concerning these models and it is also not necessary though it could pay some dividend to ascertain the models for the community that is relevant to you. These models would often be utilized in engaging the faith of an individual in a way which is constructive and in a manner that is not necessarily unfamiliar from CBT considering if they had lathed to one tenet of the faith and are utilizing this in a negative manner during the formulation. The following will consider two examples out of many which would be chosen and these are not necessarily held as the tenets for every member of these two faiths; Islam and Christianity.

Islam

The psychology of Islam as concerns the Sufi tradition was initiated during the 11 century by Al Ghazali that described the self as four elements and these were the spirit, soul, heart and the intellect. These would be set to correspond to CBT domains which would include the emotion, behavior, thoughts,and capacity for one to reflect. That would then enable the specialist, in this case, to make the western CBT concepts appear to be more acceptable.

Christianity

Christians think about the three sections of the body, spirit and the soul. The body is the natural vessel while the spirit is what is given to individuals by God to direct them and is viewed as blessed while the soul is the quintessence of that, which is our character and has the privilege of the decision of what to improve in the situation—great or malice by means of the natural vessel. Whenever utilized unhelpfully, at that point, it can result in a dualist setting where somebody that is discouraged, trusts that they have accomplished something incorrectly that has sent away the spirit and secured the soul to the body, which continues erring constantly. On the off chance that it is utilized in an accommodating setting, the therapist would have the capacity to urge the person to understand the mindcan be sick thus they can start to have depression but the soul remains and is still in touch with the spirit on some level.

Cultural factors which commonly modify the religious of spiritual expression may be a strong contribution to the perceptions and emotions of the patient. Various religions additionally have a comprehensive model for the individual and the general public which implies expert would somehow or another be sheltered when they are thinking of conduct mediations, for example, diet, practice and foundational methods of intercessions including the dealing with of family issues or the contentions as had with neighbors. The other thing is most beliefs share with CBT on the practices of reflection, the look for significance, and the journeys of self and societal improvement. For instance in the United Kingdom, with various ostensible disciples the customer might not have the inside and out learning concerning the confidence gathering and what they think concerning the brain. However, there is a component of Socratic question which would be useful for this situation. It isn't just to discover what is known yet to show where it connects to definition and could result in circumstances and disharmony which are there for change. As indicated by Padesky in great questioning, both the customer and the therapist would be amazed at that which is found and if regularly conceivable inside this zone.

Mental Models with Regards to Christianity

One might be able to show the religious confidence in a way that is commonplace to the therapists of CBT and enables them to keep working in a powerful way with beliefs considering they may have no close to home learning. There are various mental models with regards to confidence however not very many of them are clinically set. As per the spiritual care board of trustees of the Bradford District

Care trust, spirituality can be partitioned into three spaces.

1. Cognitive: these worries the associated beliefs including the unequivocally held social beliefs or musings concerning blame and disgrace. These beliefs could be conceptualized as the programmed or negative considerations as a component of the definition and they could be used as proof for testing these musings.

2. Existential: the question of what the individual feels concerning spirituality is likewise a question. This is a space which would take advantage of the feelings of the individual yet additionally into profound territories which oblige the acknowledgment and duty treatment modes and the methodologies as dependent on mending and sympathy.

3. Behavioral: what are the practices that are connected with

spiritualitylike going to scenes of
love, cooperation with others or
perusing and disguising a hallowed
content. These could have associated
issues or they may have preferences
to them, for example, social
actuation which at that point helps
with such things like detachment.

Working with that individual who is from an alternate religious and spiritual setting can represent a test for both the customer and in addition the therapist a little bit of the customers may not consider seeing a person that is outside of their confidence,however the greater part of them of them would be content with it. Then again, a portion of these distinctions can display an once in a lifetime opportunity for improvement considering the customer is required to clarify their manner of thinking and spirituality to a person that does not share the foundation, religious shorthand,and subculture. This would go towards uncovering a portion of the huge suspicions which would be investigated from a cognitive viewpoint.

With the end goal to work in this way, the therapist would likewise need to give a clarification concerning the suspicions of the customer and their spirituality. This would be past taking skeptic position considering the confidence of the customer isn't just as important and genuine for them particularly where it regards meet the objectives of treatment and could require taking a pluralist position, for example, being willing to see the truth inside the spiritual structure of the customer. The therapist may not actually need to respect the beliefs of the customer as truly evident however they may hold them delicately with the end goal to encourage what some way or another might be named restorative exchange. There may likewise be an issue not to force the manner in which that the therapist takes a gander at the word on the customer and the ones at the board talk guaranteed that the spiritual customer could be a better idea with regards to these things when contrasted with the therapist themselves.

In a model, the liberal therapist would welcome that the submitted Muslim, Christian, or the Jew is going ahead with customs that may have helped people to live in a spiritual way to create lives valuable to themselves and to other individuals. In spite of the fact that the holding of these beliefs like the current of God and the utilization of sacred text is extremely noteworthy inside the customs thus it very well may be viewed as practically evident with regards to the remedial relationship. This would be better off where the therapist is locked in inside the dialog and knows from the customer concerning the estimation of their beliefs instead of looking at them from a separation of a worldview which is now worked out.

CBT and Spirituality in Practice

At the point when people visit the therapist, they probably won't see the confidence as something which is raised regardless of whether it happens to be important to their situation. This is a result of the conviction that the authority is for the most part mainstream and does not have a spiritual conviction. It is likewise on the grounds that the therapists don't know on the way toward asking the opening inquiries. It might be viewed as that the guided revelation will go far in raising any potential issues however on the off chance that there is faltering with respect to the patients on the spiritual concerns then a methodology which is more straightforward would be the one which is generally favored.

Direction from the general medical committee set a standard in transit medical practice and individual beliefs would connect. As per the rules, one should not examine their beliefs with the patients except if they are applicable to the patients care however in doing as such it would be clear there are situations where it would be pertinent. As indicated by Murray various patients were of the conviction that the specialists would not be keen on spiritual issues despite the fact that they needed to discuss them thus various patients and carers were awkward concerning swinging to wellbeing and social administrations concerning spiritual help however on the off chance that they found the experts that were ready to talk about the requirements this ended up being extremely profitable.

There are comparative issues which were done in a report by the psychological wellness establishment as per a writing survey and specific precedents of practice relating the things which give life meaning. The report implied that the administration needs to effectively gather data on the requirements of confidence thus the clinicians were to consider the psychological wellness contemplations from a spiritual support.

Joint Workings

Consultation takes into consideration the illumination of whether beliefs or conduct are normal specifically gatherings or on the off chance that they are eccentric with regards to a bothered individual. It isn't exceptional for the misery of the patient to be influenced by seen or genuine clashes between the religious standards. The investigation of the manner in which the contentions are overseen could be of extraordinary utilize. Direction concerning what is adequate conduct may likewise be required with regards to contriving social investigations. All things considered, some are of the conviction that spirituality as a point should be disregarded so emotional well-being experts need to stick to doing CBT. All things considered, one of the normal reactions is to ask for chaplaincy to be considered. This can be a decent introductory stage and precedents would be shared on joint sessions with the clergymen were both of the authorities would take in a great deal, also the customer who is likewise profiting. There are issues that accompany chaplaincy,however. Doctor's facilities may differ with regards to the number of clergymen that are utilized and they are not going to have the capacity to see individuals with a spiritual segment to their care. They may likewise center around the in patients over the outpatients so the individual laborer may have some fundamental learning with regards to this office. In the meantime, the individual may as of now be a piece of the Christian group and not have any desire to see a minister that is of an alternate category.

Beliefs

The job of the therapist isn't expressing what is valid or not but rather it could be with the end goal to help the customers with the end goal to check whether their beliefs are in accordance with the proof and if their musings, conduct,and feeling is a piece of a keeping up plan or part of helping them to accomplish the objectives of treatment. For this situation, if a man is locked in with regards to religious conduct, for example, going to chapel, the question is whether you know whether this is useful for their depression and in the event that it very well may be encouraged.

Studies relating to Christianized CBT normally support scripture perusing, going to church and fellowship as a feature of the treatment session. However, there is no preliminary on the definition of these practices. They are considered true things and the more there are, the better. In spite of the fact that there have been individuals that read the book of scriptures as a result of their over-the-top impulsive nature of imploring with the end goal to alleviate their stresses. The issue isn't concerning the type of the manner in which they carry on as supportive churchgoing looks a great deal like unhelpful churchgoing however it is about the capacity that it is seen to have. The inquiry for this situation is whether they are asking ambiguous supplications in light of the fact that a specific petition probably won't be addressed or in the event that they are going to community gatherings as a result of a supernatural or otherworldly connect to the condition of their well-being. Try to do this with a component of interest and cooperatively without undermining your confidence. The point concerning structure is noteworthy as it isn't the shape which is the principal issue. There will be different adherents of the confidence who obviously have unhelpful practices which can be causative for wretchedness however they don't create misery. The order of quiet is one of the largeprecedents for this situation.

People fluctuate inside the religious settings however careful definition permits the unhelpful and accommodating components of their conduct and beliefs to be dismantled. Figured investigations and testing elective conduct can be valuable. Various formal religions have brought the acknowledgment for the potential for spiritual practices to be unhelpful and troubling through the improvement of their treatment modes.

One ACT approach with regards to CBT has something to offer the religious or spiritual customer. ACT originates from the social examination concerning spirituality and its techniques would incorporate the diverse methods for helping people to create on the capacities with respect to accepting and forgiving as well as increasing contact with the transcendent sense of being and becoming clearer about being more able to live in accordance with the fundamental values. These components can be identified with the spiritual system of the person since they don't originate from a specific spiritual convention.

The other component of ACT for this situation would be the accentuation on the decrease of the impact of ideas and conceptualizations of conduct. For instance, the idea of deliteralization which involves holding musings and beliefs in a light way might be valuable in situations where the discernments may compel mental adaptability and induce mental issues. Such a strategy would likewise address important confidence and conviction issues without apparently undermining them or infer a type of deserting on the legacy of a person. There are typically various styles inside some random confidence or section which would enable the therapist and their customer to think about whether as a specific conviction or spiritual practice would need to be followed in precisely the way they are following it.

Spiritually based CBT is effective for depression

Incorporating the religious beliefs of the patient into CBT allows for the relief of depression among the patients who have chronic diseases. Researchers from Duke University found the approach seems tobe as effective as the conventional means of Cognitive Behavioral Therapy. According to Dr. Harold Koenig from the Duke University Medical Center, the integration of the client beliefs into CBT does not tend to reduce its effectiveness especially for those clients that are spiritually oriented. The researchers are of the belief that the incorporation of spirituality may help to make psychotherapy more acceptable to the spiritually oriented patients that have depression or chronic diseases.

What makes religiously integrated Cognitive Behavioral Therapy unique is the explicit use of the religious beliefs of the client so as to replace and identify those unhelpful thoughts. Therapists that are experienced in the integration of religion into psychotherapy led the sessions for Cognitive Behavioral Therapy. A lot of the patients happened to be Christian though some have been able to receive religious CBT adapted to their faiths. At the end of the therapy, you may find that patients who identify as highly religious have a somewhat greater improvement in their depression scores with religiously oriented CBT as compared to conventional CBT. Could that mean that religious CBT is the better choice for the patients that are suffering from depression or does it mean that depression has a spiritual basis and responds better to religious treatment methods?

The spiritual dimension of depression literature on caring for the whole person considers that human suffering is not only cognitive or emotional but also spiritual. Though getting consensus on the definitions of existential distress is still a bit elusive. One significant step toward a consensus which is usable would be agreeing on the meaning the terms which are commonly utilized for describing existential, spiritual and emotional distress. For example, the emotional dimension of the concerns of the patients could be said to refer to the feelings, the existential dimension to the conditions of existence and the spiritual to the meaningful connection to something which is transcendent or bigger than us. Acceptance pertaining the distinctions drawn by this vocabulary can assist the clinicians and researchers to ascertain when definite concerns like a sense of isolation share two or three of the dimensions and are thus not capable of adequate description by only one. One obvious relationship between the existential and spiritual dimensions as understood in these terms would be that spirituality may function to give a response to the concerns related to an existential nature. One additional relevant distinction is that which is highlighted by Charles Taylor between the voluntarily, optional ways of finding and investing meaning in an imminent frame in the same way as one would find in the nature of art and experiences which would lay claim on one because of their significance.

Fostering good spirituality

Consider some of the ways healthy spirituality would mean a helpful response to the existential concerns which are amplified or distorted in depression when it comes to domains such as hope, meaning, purpose, and autonomy in relation to authority. Coming to these transcendent answers is rather facilitated by spirituality which is engaging and transformative as opposed to static. With respect to hope and its underpinnings when a loss or serious illness shakes the trust of the individual in God, they can start to despair and become quite cynical. The patients that ground their ultimate hopes in the ideals like truth, compassion, or justice could also be vulnerable when it comes to despair if they happen to be disillusioned by the individuals that have represented particular ideals within their lives. Whatever the objects of their particular faith the patients that have lost hope need spirituality which is integrated as opposed to ambivalent.

As such a survivor of trauma, for example, needs to reconstruct what would be the fragmented perspective of their world. A spirituality which sustains hope is something that is real and can be attained to the individual not only when they are in a comfortable setting but also when in crisis in their life. This would otherwise be termed as the courage for an individual to be. A number of individuals bring into treatment their search for purpose and the meaning of their crises. For example, an atheist that loses their child to cancer could bring into question whether their life has a purpose. Whatever their perspective, the patients that are searching for meaning need spirituality which is particularly attuned as opposed to impulsive or based on their particular needs. Being attuned to worship and prayer can assist the patient to maintain perspective and become grounded.

Patients also deal with struggles that have particular moral elements. These are set according to the worldview. In a number of ways the understanding people have of God and the universe is what shapes their commitment to justice. Philosophical or religious modes of thought would guide the way that people make decisions. Religious standards and regulations articulate what is right and wrong and they provide alternatives for how to deal with failure in morals such as confessing of sins and repentance then making amends.

Faith-based groups and organizations assist with the supporting of virtues which would be basic to clinical work, humility, and honesty and caring. In spite of the indifference in the worldviews, the patients that have moral concerns require spirituality which is otherwise mature as opposed to developmentally held back. Healthcare professionals can assist the patients who are mature to view the advantages of selecting mature connections and intimacy through means of forgiveness over childish satisfaction when it comes to maintaining control or of being in the right. The worldviews of those who are religious and those who are not differ especially when it comes to their relationship with God. The non-religious question if there is an authority that one can trust and take direction from or does one have to rely only on themselves. Whatever the worldviews that you may have there are particular advantages to feeling protected and loved as opposed to being entirely alone or pointless on the earth. The therapist can assist patients to look at what kind of intimacy they want with God and others on earth. Interpersonal therapy methods and attention are to the ways the spiritual community would consider the dynamics of connections with other people.

Spiritually Integrated Treatment

What would be the designation of spiritually oriented methods in the assessment of the therapist, not to mention the way they formulate and then treat? The image below shows a basic framework for intervention at the interface between spiritual, emotional and existential distress within the scope of the main concerns of the depressed individuals in order to initiate a healthy type of spirituality. Though insight oriented and cognitive behavior type of approaches may assist individuals that are depressed distinguish between the distressing emotions from their basis in life experiences, the spiritually oriented interventions would assist them to utilize their knowledge and experience.

Table 1: A framework for intervention.

	Identity	Hope	Meaning/purpose	Morality	Connection
Emotional (I feel...)	As if I don't know who I am	Despairing	Directionless	Guilty	Lonely
Insight oriented CBT					
Existential (I experience the world as if...)	there is nothing special about me	Life is hopeless	Life is meaningless	I am guilty	I am alone
Spiritually oriented Rx					
Spiritual (I'm inclined to believe...)	God is punishing/ignoring me	No ultimate basis for hope exists	The universe is random and empty	No ultimate basis for morality exists	I am rejected by God/ultimately alone

Source: https://www.hindawi.com/journals/drt/2012/124370/tab1/

From the stress-diathesis viewpoint, there may be conditions which show vulnerability to a mood which is depressed in that they are different in their etiologies and therapeutic considerations. Some of these entail demoralization, bipolar disorders, adjustment problems, personality related depression, not to mention complicated grief and general unhappiness.

The main concern of people that are suffering from these problems and their existential dimensions are most likely going to be different. Patients who have a hard time keeping hope because their experience of life is fragmented and are cynical when in despair would be thought to benefit from achieving a more integrated form of spirituality through exploring the hurt which is unresolved. As such, CBT which brings their main beliefs in line with their experience and interpersonal therapy or direction focuses on doubts concerning trusting God or the direction their lives are taking.Depressed individuals that struggle in finding their sense of meaning or who feel that their life lost its purpose would have the expectation to benefit from meaning-centered therapy and meditation. Patients that are concerned with moral queries like those who feel overwhelmed by guilt when they are depressed would be expected to gain advantage from forgiveness thus promoting therapy and positive psychology concerning the aspirational virtues like patience and love. Those patients that have existential worries center on their relationship to God and those who feel rejected and depressed would be expected to gain from feeling accepted by the same higher authority.

The means to this end therapeutically speaking would include psycho-dynamically oriented treatment which is set on the distorted object relations, not to mention interpersonal therapy concentrated on their relationship to a higher power. The approaches which are spiritually oriented which address the problems like the relationship to God could also result in addressing concerns to other designated areas like hope and identity. The individual that feels loved by God for example and constantly surrendered by his will is going to be less prone to be distracted and pray to smaller gods figuratively speaking. These include power and pleasure which are not permanent and would eventually leave the person lost.

There are a number of places where integrated treatment would be given from the office of the therapist in a hospital to an assigned chaplain within a clinic that is faith-based. Each location comes with its opportunities and problems for referral and collaboration. In the most straightforward of these scenarios, the therapist may provide a direct link to the issue though they would limit their discussion to the psychological dimension. As an example, he or she may focus on the way that the problem is interfering with the care of the patient or they may focus on the anger of the patient toward God by examining their relationship with other authority figures in the life of the patient.

The other potential approach would be clarifying the psychological and spiritual elements of the issue suggesting the resources when it comes to dealing with the spiritual and considering working with an external source like a religious community. This may include enlisting the help of a member of the clergy in order to assist with the spiritual needs. It may also pertain including referrals to programs which integrate the emotions and beliefs such as spiritually centered programs oriented in CBT.

The third method would entail the therapist addressing the problem from an indirect setting using the philosophy of the patient within the treatment. That may mean exploring means that the patient would make a better use of what they have along with their traditions. In this case, it would be advisable for the therapists to consider the way different perspectives of the world and spiritual views address the existential issues including how the patient sees themselves. In the Christian setting, each individual is rooted in sin and needs to be transformed and heal through the power of God. When it comes to the Buddhist tradition each person is part of the universe.

They may be unhappy but they are not able to enlighten themselves solely. The secular western view maintains that everyone is limited by their individual bias and is alone and cannot live with integrity owing to the capitalist settings of the society.

The final method would be addressing the problem in a direct manner with the use of a shared perspective from the agreement of the therapist on the importance of hope considering the world perspective or caring community to the use of values, beliefs within the treatment. This method needs some attention towards the boundary and consent problems. Several factors are relevant when it comes to deciding the approaches which are to be implemented. The first would be the need of the patient for adjustment, growth and even problem-solving. That would then affect the impact the nature, objectives and the relevant timing of the objective. This could be the psychological insight into a pattern which is maladaptive or the resolution of a conflict.

That, in turn, affects the degree concerning the direct support which is required and the interpersonal closeness that is appropriate. Some of the additional factors include the existential considerations like that which is related to hope or identity and the importance of spirituality within the life of the patient. However, the framework of the integrated treatment as suggested increases the number of challenging queries. For one, which aspect of the condition of the depressed individual needed to have priority and which of them were to get a spiritually oriented approach? The other query relates to the importance of the therapist and the patient'sworldview when it comes to the formulation of goals within spiritual care.

Chapter5: Benefits of Cognitive Behavioral Therapy

Cognitive Behavioral Therapy can be as effective as any form of medication. However, how it is done and what it is being used for can determine the success rate of it. Studies have shown that it is not successful or suitable for everyone; that been said, the success stories have shown a number of benefits, advantages, or pros when treating mental disorders such as OCD, panic disorders, and PTSD among others. Let us now examine the benefits of CBT; it is important to note that these advantages do not simply apply to those with mental disorders but also those who have shown symptoms of negative behavior, addiction, anxiety, depression, and such. It is also important to note that advantages of Cognitive Behavioral Therapy are co-dependent and rely on the effectiveness of the treatment and how well the patients respond to the sessions.

1. It can be used in place of medication

Small non-threatening diseases have shown over the years that not everyone is into medication or injections. Some people would rather take up natural remedies such as honey, lemon, and ginger mix to cure a cold than get over the counter drugs. Likewise, when it comes to treating mental disorders, medication can fail or not be successful with the patient. Because Cognitive Behavioral Therapy involves therapy through talking, it may have a higher success rate with people who do not react well with medication.

According to researchers, CBT has been proven to have longer lasting effects; this is according to a famous study by the Johns Hopkins Bloomberg School of Public Health, Oxford University and University College London which analyzed data from 101 clinical trials aimed at comparing multiple types of medication and talk therapy. The results showed that among all different types of talk therapy examined inclusive of self-help, psychodynamic psychotherapy, and CBT, CBT was found to be the most effective with the least side effects too. The research concluded that although medication is effective in treating mental disorders, cognitive therapy has the advantage because it gives what medication cannot, it gives education that has longer lasting effects.

Medication is known to have some serious side effects on the body both physically and mentally; some peoples' bodies can actually reject medication. This is the case especially with young people and children; though medication tends to work faster than therapy it could be a healthier alternative if the medication is rejected. If you are conscious about giving your child medication or are not sure about it, CBT is a great alternative that will not only help your child but also you as you can share the sessions once in a while. What is more is that it can be paired with medication to help treat disorders; this does not necessarily mean that the results will be better or that recovery will come quicker. However, it can help with resistance and can give you improved results with patients who are not responding to either.

2. Time efficiency

Many forms of treatment for disorders take different amounts of time to accomplish; while some take a couple of days or a few hours others take years for one to fully recover. With disorders, it is usually the latter; even with medication, it can take many years to fully recover from a disorder. Cognitive Behavioral Therapy is a form of therapy that provides a relatively short time to complete. Unlike other forms of talk therapies, CBT can be completed in a short time whereby the patient. With regular weekly sessions, a patient is able to complete their therapy sessions in just twelve to sixteen weeks.It seems impossible but it is actually a very systematic form of treatment. It is a manual based system of strategies that are empirically supported and define many specific, countable, and achievable targets or goals. This process facilitates the treatment process without delaying which allows the therapist to make maximum use of the time. This is better than a normal therapy session that could have you going on for a while.Once treatment has been established, the therapiststarts a review for over a determined amount of time; this scrutiny of the progress of the patient enables both the patient and therapist to make informed decisions and change depending on the results being collected. These changes are to be used to prevent relapsing and implore the patient to take control. Finally, the therapist will gradually take steps back to allow the patient to fly solo and will be present less and less as the patient continues to trust themselves to improve behavior or stop their addictive participation. Not only is this convenient for your time, but it is also reasonably generous on your wallet. That way, you do not end up in debt trying to improve yourself; it also gives you well enough time to recover on your own and practice what you have been taught.

3. **Flexibility**

As we have already established, Cognitive Behavioral Therapy is used to a variety of disorders from PTSD to eating disorders. This is the first form of flexibility that it takes; it can be used for people with and without mental disorders such as eating disorders, PTSD, OCD, gambling addiction, alcohol dependency, and drug dependency among others.

The second form of flexibility comes about because CBT is talk therapy. It has the power to be used on a variety of platforms. For example, it can be used for In-patient patients as they are receiving medication in the hospital; it can also be used on out-patient patients who can schedule appointments as recommended by the hospital with the help of their family members. Another form of flexibility is the fact that CBT is available almost anywhere including hospitals, recovery centers, and even personal therapists. Most hospitals come with their own trained therapists but if you feel like you are more comfortable with a different therapist, all you need to do is find a trained one. What is more, it can also be paired with other forms of therapy and of course with medication. This is mostly applicable to people with severe disorders and people who have been diagnosed for a long time and take time to respond to each treatment individually. The best form of flexibility for CBT is that it is effective in both individual sessions and group sessions; for when you need to meet your individual needs and for when you need support from people who know what it is like to be in your shoes. This is especially great for young adults and children who need the support of friends and family or would rather not be alone during their sessions. The flexibility of CBT ensures that each patient from different backgrounds, disorders, and generally lives are able to receive the treatment that they deserve.

4. Collaborative approach

Unlike other forms of therapy, Cognitive Behavioral Therapy allows for a collaborative approach. The collaborative approach or collaborative empiricism is a systematic process where the therapist and the patient work together. They work together to accomplish common goals which are set by both of them at the beginning of the session by both of them. This method is important because it is used to uncover the thoughts, beliefs, and concerns which will then be used to treat the emotional and behavioral disorders. The role of the therapist becomes to develop, promote, and maintain therapeutic collaboration with the patient.

Other forms of therapy usually involve the patient talking about his or her concerns then the therapist telling him or her what it means, and suggesting approaches to take; basically telling them what to do. This method has been proven to be effective and on paper, there is nothing wrong with it. CBT, however, brings on a different approach to therapy; the therapy session is a collaborative process. The patient reveals information about themselves and the disorder; the therapist learns what the patient wants to change or what their concerns are. After this, the therapist helps the patient accomplish this through the information he or she has gathered about the life and disorder of the patient. The therapist will not tell the patient what to do or what not to do but rather will encourage the patient to talk it out and guide them towards taking an action that they (the patient) feel will be beneficial to themselves. This type of therapy is ultimately beneficial because when the patient finishes the treatment they will be independent enough to deal with the stresses that will come. It also allows the patient to thrive in stressful situations without constantly needing approval, or confirmation from the therapist.

5. **Structured nature**

Cognitive Behavioral Therapy is a structured program that involves arranged and structures sessions. While each session addresses each patient individually in order to maximize the output, there is a standard structure that can be used for individuals and groups to receive the same results. During the first check-in, the patient and therapist discuss the basic structure of what will be their sessions.

Cognitive therapy usually involves a series of phases inclusive of noting problem areas, setting goals and targets for the period allocated for the treatment, check-ins by the therapist, adjustment of strategies by both therapist and patient depending on the results gotten from reaching for the goals, and finally the 'let go' process by the therapist as the treatment continues.

A great thing with structure is that it can be easily put into self-help books, audio tapes, articles, etc. making this information available to anyone and everyone. Structure is also important in case of relapse, though it is rare; relapse can be treated with going back to the basics which are easy to do if you have some form of structural procedure that you have been following. Structure is also important because it helps to provide motivation to the patients to complete the program; small victories in the form of steps completed motivates the patient to keep at it and not quit midway. The structured nature of this type of therapy is also good because it allows the patient to make targets or goals that are structured and achievable with the guide of the therapist. Ultimately, this is also helpful to the patient in everyday life; you will realize that patients who have undergone this type of treatment will have a more structural approach to life; especially when it comes to solving problems, dealing with disagreements, and expressing their emotions. It is the ultimate advantage that turns anyone into a more structured person.

6. Skills and strategies

Cognitive Behavioral Therapy is the type of therapy that lets you tap into who you really are. After several sessions, you realize that through trying to work on your issues and disorders you acquire skills and strategies that can overall help you and others. These strategies and skills are functional in that they help you achieve your overall goals during the therapy sessions even when you are not physically in the session. What is even better is that these skills and strategies can be used by the patient to handle future stresses and difficulties even after they have finished their sessions. These skills are also important for when the patient is about to relapse; it prevents relapsing and improves behavior. This also applies to people with addictions; gambling and dependencies.

Moreover, people who join their family members or friends for support and group sessions acquire skills that help in the long run to not only understand the patient's behavior but also to deal with the patient's behavior. Most people affected by a friend or family member's disorder usually have no idea what to do in the case of the attack; this leads to 'crashing and burning' by the person when an attack is taking place. This type of reaction is not met positively by the afflicted person and it can lead them to feel even more ashamed, confused and angry. CBT, because it is flexible equips people who care for those with mental disorders the skills they need to support them and teaches them the various approaches to when the patient is experiencing an attack and especially for when the patient is about to (or has already) relapsed. Finally, the skills and strategies acquired by both parties can help the patient and other people to help those in need. Once successfully undergone the treatment, a patient's determination of sticking to what they have learned can eventually allow them to help others in need. In fact, a stud shows that some of the best therapists and counselors are people who were once suffering from the same problem.

7. Support

Cognitive Behavioral Therapy is a great way to receive support from others who have been in your place or at least are sharing the same experience. Because CBT can be done in group sessions and can be done with sessions that involve your friends and family, it proves a support system for you individually. Support helps patients to keep at the sessions and prevents relapsing. This is possible in tow main ways; first, the patient will do everything in their power not to disappoint those who are supporting them. If they feeling like there is someone there to support them because they genuinely care, then it motivates them to keep this person feeling proud and happy for their accomplishments. Second, support in the form of attending family sessions equips those affected with the skills to stop the patient from relapsing through identifying patterns and behaviors. This knowledge can be used to reassure the patient of the journey they are taking together and prevent relapsing into the behavior or addiction.

Overall, these sessions are mainly to help others such as (family and friends) to understand your condition and help you deal with it. Support also helps both you and others in your position to know that they are not alone in their struggle and that anybody and everybody is accepted in the community. Knowing that there is someone interested in their recovery helps the patients keep at it and change their negative behavior; it also lets them know that despite their disorder, there are people who love them and will stick by them. This is very beneficial to the patient and will allow them to recover even faster. Studies show that patients who join support groups or are accompaniedby a friend or family member, or have people who are actively involved in their recovery process tend to have a higher resistance to relapsing. Plus, they have a somewhat stronger will and will go out of their way to make progress.

8. Self-Esteem

For most people, the underlying problem with their disorder is low self-esteem. It may have happened while they were young or even when they were adults but low self-esteem can lead to a lot of disorders. How much you love yourself and like who you are can say a lot about you and explains many things about your life. Low self-esteem can be associated with many problems including disorders, dependencies, short temper, violence, and even bullying. This is especially prevalent among young children; if one is not careful, it is very easy to lead a child into having low self-esteem simply by the way we speak around them, and what we say about them to others. If not remedied, this child will grow up self-conscious and always bottling things up. This can lead to the child turning to drugs, alcohol, gambling, and other forms of dependencies in order to feel wanted. What is worse is that they could develop disorders; one common one as a result of low self-esteem is eating disorders where in trying to be thinner or fatter the person develops complications such as bulimia and anorexia.

Through CBT, patients are able to work on their problems by focusing on them and finding a solution or solutions. Through this, patients raise their self-esteem because through making these decisions, they trust their judgments and when they turn out to be successful they gain confidence in themselves. As they find answers to their problems, they allow themselves to grow and become confident enough to conquer the disorders. A higher self-esteem allows patients to trust themselves more, manage their behavior, and also help others who are going through the same. A higher self-esteem also shows people with dependencies that they do not need to be depended to be acceptable to the community. They find themselves through the treatment and accept themselves through the support of friends and family.

9. Change of thought

Scientific studies have shown that thoughts are the driving force of our behavior; how we react to information, news, and situations is entirely based on our thoughts. If our thoughts lead us into thinking that the situation is aggressive, the output behavior will be defensive and to some extent even negative. In the same way, if our thoughts show us that the situation is polite, calm, and controlled then the output behavior will be that of a calm person, in control with self-confidence and self-respect. This is applicable to all people whether you have a mental disorder or not.

Cognitive Behavioral Therapy is a great way for patients to change their way of thinking and overall change their behavior,especially in aggressive situations. With any mental disorder comes a persistent, 'normal' and almost unchangeable way of thinking that it more negative than it is positive or even neutral. Negative thoughts are extremely dangerous because they can cause relapsing, self-hate, and to some extent self-harm. CBT sessions teach the patients how to turn their negative thoughts and attitudes into positive ones. This is a truly remarkable advantage that cannot be achieved by medicine and some other forms of therapy. A change of thought and attitude towards life helps the patient to manage their behavior and motivate them into working harder on their sessions. It also helps them make positive and realistic changes and decisions in their lives. For example, a patient who would eat because they are depressed would now love for more positive ways to deal with it such as talking to someone. The change in though greatly affects the way the [patient behaves during confrontations, negative situation, and disagreements. After several sessions, you will realize that the patient will be able to control emotions well and approach each situation with a positive attitude even when faced in a confrontation or disagreement. Seeing the positive side of things is also an ultimate morale boost to continue with the sessions and allow the will improve the self-esteem of the person in general.

10. Anger management

Controlling your emotions, even as an adult is a tedious task and somehow impossible. For most people, emotional awareness and control is something they have failed to achieve; people often feel many emotions at once and will have great trouble deducing what to feel and what to ignore. This, of course, leads to confusion and with confusion comes disaster. People who are not in control of their emotions often exhibit mood swings, and over aggression. For most people, this feeling of not being in control leads to aggression, and violence all fueled up by anger. Anger takes over every other emotion when it comes to a battle of feelings.

Mentally ill patients usually have a problem with controlling and managing their anger. Feelings of guilt, shame, and confusion can easily turn into anger for the patient with a mental illness. Cognitive Behavioral Therapy can be used to address underlying issues of emotional trauma that causes anger in patients. It teaches patients different ways of dealing with their emotions and how to control how they respond with their emotions. This, in turn, helps them manage anger and only use it to respond when it is absolutely necessary.

CBT offers anger management training in the form of mindfulness training which trains you on being mindful of behavior which turns negative thoughts into positive ones, cognitive restructuring of dysfunctional thoughts, distress tolerance training which teaches the patient how to steer away from anger, emotion regulation training that teaches emotional restraint and output, and finally assertiveness skill building for building up assertiveness. Management of anger is a key part of recovery for the patients with mental disorders because through controlling their behavior, patients gain a more positive output in how they interact with people.

11. Communication skills

People with mental disorders usually have a hard time maintaining relationships with others. The biggest hindrance to this is the communication; without communication, it is difficult to maintain relationships with others. This is because communication in the key to talking to others and sharing thoughts, experiences, promises, and such. Most relationships actually end up failing due to miscommunication or a complete lack of it. When people want to share their thoughts, beliefs, and values they use communication to do so. Unfortunately, if you are unable to communicate your message effectively, then people are not able to understand you. Being unable to have your thoughts and opinions understood is extremely frustrating especially if you are trying to ask for help.

With Cognitive Behavioral Therapy, patients are able to learn how to communicate with others both verbally and without the use of words. It teaches patients how to communicate their feelings well without getting angry or feeling ashamed, or shy away from people and relationships. Great communication is not only about talking but also listening. CBT sessions are helpful in teaching patients how to listen to others and how their needs are as important as those of others. For addicts, communication skills are important because they allow you to communicate what your thoughts on addiction and how you ended up there. You will be able to express yourself to family and friends and even help others understand how you ended. You will be able to ask for help when you feel like you are about to relapse and listen to others as they share their experiences in the same situation. Communication skills are mostly developed during cognitive therapy group sessions with both family and others who need therapy.

12. Coping skills

Another cause of mental disorders that is common especially among young children is the inability to cope with stressful situations such as grief, change, or trauma. These situations are stressful and so only a few people are able to deal with them accordingly; others turn to alcohol, hard drugs, and even toxic behaviors such as violence. Those who cannot deal with it well or badly end up bottling their emotions which if done for a long time can lead to serious mental behaviors. As humans, we all need some form of coping mechanism to help us get through stressful situations. Without these coping mechanisms, we would not be able to survive loss, sadness, and grief. Unfortunately, very few people have been able to tame their demons with positive coping skills; more than often both children and adults end up with less than friendly habits.

Cognitive Behavioral Therapy teaches patients how to deal with stressful situations; through these sessions, they are able to learn how to open up instead of bottling things up. This, in the long run, teaches patients how to behave in confrontations, how to express dissatisfaction in situations, and also how to handle disagreements with people, especially in relationships without having to cause a break or split in the relationship.

For people who have had dependencies and addiction, CBT sessions help them tap into who they really are and encourages them to come up with their own coping mechanisms for dealing with cravings and withdrawals. This form of therapy is also useful for people who have relatives and friends with mental disorders. Because they are human, people affected may also crash and burn when faced with the reality of their loved one being tortured by their condition. Group sessions that involve family help them to find healthy ways to cope with situations that are far from happy.

13. Preventing relapse

It is popularly known that patients who suffer from mental diseases are often prone to relapse; it is quite common even when on medication. A great advantage of Cognitive Behavioral Therapy is that it provides patients with not only the skills to deal with everyday situations but also equips them with the tools to prevent relapse. It is a broad type of therapy that teaches patients to deal with behavior and stressful situations while also helping them identify their problem areas and recognize their patterns. Through being able to recognize patterns, patients are able to identify symptoms of an upcoming relapse and will take many great steps to prevent this. This is a very attractive feature as compared to medication which does not allow for such.

Cognitive therapy though it is doubted is actually helpful to people who are treating their dependencies and addiction. Most forms of treatment use medication to prevent addicts from relapsing, this is helpful but at the same time, it can be quite risky. Some people end up getting addicted to the very medication that is supposed to help them get clean. In one of the first steps of CBT known as dysfunctional analysis, patients of dependency identify the circumstances, thoughts, and feelings that led them to drug abuse in the first place. This is very useful because it helps to identify situations that could lead to relapsing. The skills they acquire are more useful because they can also help those who have been there or are there once they finish their sessions and continue in their sobriety journey.

14. Addiction

Even if you do not have a mental disorder, Cognitive Behavioral Therapy can be useful to you. Research has shown scientific-based results of CBT to help treat drug dependencies such as alcohol dependence and opioid. What is more is that it can be used to help people quit smoking and even gambling. Studies have shown that treatments associated with CBT equip people who are addicted to a particular behavior or drug with the skills to stop or reduce their dependency. These coping skills have been found to be highly effective during withdrawals, and when cravingfor the drug. The result of using CBT to treat problematic behaviors such as gambling has been proven to be more effective than when using control treatments. In fact, patients who undergo CBT for such behavior and addictions are less likely to relapse than people who undergo control treatment procedures.

People with mental disorders do expel some symptoms of being addicted to their behaviors. For example, when the opportunity to socialize with others presents itself, most patients will not attempt to form relationships or even have conversations because they are addicted to what they know; feelings of confusion and solitude. It is a comfort zone but in a realsense, it is an addiction to the behavior. Because it is so involving, CBT helps people who are addicted to both behavior and drugs to find healthier mechanisms to deal with the thing that is causing them to turn to addictions. This is as a result of the sessions being more involving of the patient and the fact that they help uncover feelings and thoughts that led to addiction in the first place.

15. Anxiety

Anxiety is one of those diseases that you are probably ignoring or unaware of. Every day, people are suffering from anxiety and are not even aware of it; the brush it off as jitters or nervousness. While these are actual conditions, anxiety is persistent and can show up at any time; you could be sleeping in the middle of the night then suddenly wake up with a feeling of uneasiness like something is about to happen or that something already happened. There is medication that is administered for anxiety but one would first have to get diagnosed by a professional. The medication is helpful but unfortunately, like other forms of medication, it does not work for everyone.

There is substantial evidence that Cognitive Behavioral Therapy is effective in reducing anxiety among people. Studies have shown that CBT works extremely well as a natural remedy for anxiety because it features self-monitoring symptoms, psycho-education about the nature of anxiety and fear, cognitive restructuring, somatic exercises, weaning from ineffective safety signals, image and in vivo exposure to feared stimuli, and finally relapse prevention. This knowledge and practices allow people with anxiety to learn how to control it and even reduce if not completely eradicate the symptoms. Managing anxiety can surprisingly help prevent the development of any other mental disorders which improves your mental health and keeps you looking at the positive side of life. Anxiety is prevalent in people who have chosen to let go of their dependencies, it is a common symptom of withdrawals. While medication is useful, CBT sessions are also quite helpful in managing this type of anxiety.

16. Depression

Depression is another of the disorders that are hard to identify; people go as far as saying that it might not be depression but just a feeling of sadness. As we have already established, Cognitive Behavioral Therapy is one of the best-known forms of treatment for depression. Studies have shown that CBT sessions help the patient to reduce and eradicate symptoms of depression such as helplessness, low motivation, anger, and emotional trauma, not to mention relapsing. Cognitive Behavioral Therapy works extremely well in reducing depression because it causes a change in thoughts (as mentioned above) that fan the fire that is negative thinking. CBT is a suitable replacement for depression medication as it has been proven to give better results especially in handling postpartum depression. What's more is that a variant of Cognitive Behavioral Therapy known as preventive cognitive therapy when paired with antidepressants has been found to help patients who were experiencing continuous depression. A study conducted in 2018 showed 289 participants being randomly assigned PCT sessions along with antidepressants, antidepressants alone, and PCT sessions only. The results showed that PCT paired with antidepressants was first rate as compared to antidepressants alone and PC alone.

Chapter 6: Most optimal CBT practices

There are some cognitive behavioral practices that help to modify a patient's behavioral patterns and strip them of negative thoughts. Through his modification, patients are able to replace their negative thoughts with positive ones which is an ultimate change in their personality. This section observes the most optimal CBT practices that have shown valid results.

1. **Journaling**

    Journaling or self-monitoring is a practice of Cognitive Behavioral Therapy that allows patients undergoing the therapy treatment to write down their moods and thoughts in a process that allows one to gather information about the behaviors and thoughts. Thought records are designed to determine the validity of thoughts from a patient. This journal includes many factors on mood and behavior such as the time of the mood, how you responded to it, how intense it was, and of course how you chose to deal with it.

The thought record is useful to both the patient and therapist in identifying maladaptive thought patterns and emotional tendencies. The journal describes them vividly then during the session, the therapist conducts a discussion with the patient to find out the different ways in which behavior of the patient is affected, how to change, adapt and cope with these effects. This record is important because it helps to change beliefs on a logical level, that way the patient is able to deal with changes in mood and behavior not only physically but mentally; it helps to change the mindset. For example, upon receiving negative feedback from a supervisor, an intern could do a thought record of their reaction (which is most likely negative) to evaluate the evidence for and against the thought. Through this, the intern is able to come up with more balanced thoughts such as admitting that they were at fault. The journal entries are simple as shown here.

2. Behavioral Experiments

When it comes to Cognitive Behavioral Therapy, there are some behavioral experiments that are designed to tests the thoughts of the patient. This process of experimentation includes experiencing, observing or watching, reflecting, and planning. This is a self-done process that explores the patient to write down the results and evaluate the information. First, the patient experiences the behavior that they want to change, then they observe or watch what happens when they perform the test or experiment, next they will reflect on the results and plan their strategies for the next time they experience the same. For example, you may decide to perform a behavioral experiment to test the thought 'if I criticize myself after overeating I will overeat less often vs. if I talk to myself with kindness after overeating I will overeat less often.' In order to do this, the patient would have attempted each approach on different occasions and monitor what happens in the case of overeating. This is because it gives you the objective feedback of what works more effectively in reducing your overeating; either being kind to you or criticizing yourself. Such an experiment is also useful in countering thoughts of presumption such as being kind to yourself mean that you have given yourself a free pass to eat as much as you like and that you will not be able to control yourself.

3. Pleasurable activities

Upon hearing it you would not think that this is a successful Cognitive Behavioral Therapy practice; however, it is one of the most effective ones till date. This type of practice is especially useful to people with depression but it can be used by anyone. It is helpful because it helps patients engage in activities that they would not normally engage in due to their behaviors. The process is to first identify a low-frequency behavior such as social interaction or conversation starting. Once the behavior has been identified, the patient finds time during the week to schedule a behavior to increase its frequency for example attending a party or going out on a date. You could say that it is a way of reintroducing rewarding behaviors into the routine of the patient.

The patient has the option of scheduling at least one pleasant activity per day; one that they would not normally do or to schedule an activity that gives them a sense of accomplishment, competence, or some form of mastery. The advanced version would be to schedule three activities, one for morning, lunch, and evening; doing the activities produces positive emotions to stop the patient from thinking negative.

4. Situation-exposure hierarchies

This is another form journaling that is interesting and will allow the patient to learn more about themselves. The situation exposure hierarchies involve putting things you would normally avoid under any circumstances on a list in hierarchical order. For each item on the list, the patient should use a scale from one to ten, ten being the thing avoided most. For example, a patient who has social anxiety will make a list of activities that they are likely to avoid ranging from asking someone out on a date (at the top) all the way to asking for directions from a stranger (at the bottom). Another patient with an eating disorder might make a list of foods they avoid ranging from ice cream (at the top of the list) all the way to full-fat flavored yogurt (at the bottom of the list). In this case, the 10 would be the ice-cream and asking someone out on a date while the 0 would be full-fatyogurt and asking for directions from a stranger. Once you have your list, the idea is to work your way through the list eliminating each at every stop from lowest to highest. The process can vary on speed depending on how comfortable you are at the next point; experiment with each item several times over a period of time before moving on to the next one.

5. Imagery-based exposure

This is a great strategy of Cognitive Behavioral Therapy that is specifically useful in preventing relapsing. One common version of imagery involves calling the mind to a recent memory that provoked a negative reaction or an emotional one from the patient. In this strategy, the patient brings back the memory in full details such as what was happening, what was said, how it was said, where it happened, and how they reacted. The patient would be able to identify what emotions and thoughts they experienced during the situation and more importantly what their behavioral urges were. For example, did they want to run, cry, or talk back? Etc. If the patient experiences imagery exposure for a long time, they will be able to reduce their levels of stress until it is half of what it was at the moment of the situation. Imagery based exposure helps to counteract relapsing of the patient; this is because it helps to turn painful and intrusive memories into ones that are less likely to trigger relapsing. It is also helpful in reducing avoidance coping; because when a person is less distresses by intrusive memories, they are able to choose healthier actions in dealing with situations.

6.   Cognitive restructuring

This is the process of learning to identify and challenge maladaptive or irrational thoughts commonly known as cognitive distortions which are commonly associated with any mental disorder. Once the patient identifies the inaccurate views or distortions about the world that they are holding on to, they begin to learn about how the distortion took root in your mind and why they have chosen to believe and hold on to it. When the patient accepts that the belief is damaging to who they are, they can begin to challenge it. For example, if you believe that you must eat less to have a beautiful body but you have eaten more than you had planned, you will obviously feel bad about yourself. The cognitive restructuring comes when refuse to accept this faulty belief that is the root of your negative thoughts and self-hate.

Instead, you can take this opportunity to think about what it really means to have a beautiful body that you love and is comfortable in. during this process, the patient will consider views of a 'beautiful body' that they had not considered before. Cognitive restructuring employs many different strategies such as thought recording and guided imagery.

7. Socratic questioning

Socratic questioning is another practice of Cognitive Behavioral Therapy that was inspired but the Greek philosopher Socrates. It is based on the practice of disciplined and thoughtful dialogue; Socrates believed that the disciplined practice of thoughtful questioning helps the learner to examine ideas in a logical manner and be able to validate those ideas. As used in Cognitive Behavioral Therapy, the questioning allows the therapist to challenge the patient's self-awareness, focus their attention on the definition of the problem, expose the belief system of the patient, and finally change the irrational beliefs while showing the patient their negative cognitive processes. Although it appears simple, Socratic questioning is rigorous and intense; the therapist fakes ignorance about a certain topic and instead allows the patient to reveal as much information about the subject. In doing so, the patient is able to recognize contradictions and so they would be able to correct their own incomplete or inaccurate ideas about the world. The process leads to progressively greater truth and accuracy.

8. Relaxed breathing

Relaxed breathing is useful to anyone in any situation; in fact, therapists and doctors recommend doing breathing exercises at least once per day, every day. This is because it allows you to think better, clear your mind, and evaluate situations differently. This is yet another practice that people often shun even though it has proven to have great results. Though it is not specific to Cognitive Behavioral Therapy it is still very helpful. There are many different ways of relaxing and bringing regularity to your breath. Bringing regularity to calm your breath allows the patient to tackle their problems from a balanced place which in turn facilities effective and rational decision making from the patient even in stressful situations that they should normally fail at or react negatively too. For example, taking the situation of the intern who receives negative feedback from the supervisor; if the intern was to take a moment to relax, and evaluate the situation, they would be able to make informed and logical decisions rather than emotionally charged ones. This prevents an ultimate disaster of negative reaction; this technique is especially effective for patients with OCD, depression, and panic disorder. The best thing about this practice is that it can be practiced with or without the guidance of a therapist.

9. Statements to counteract the negative

This is a practice that pairs well with journaling and cognitive restructuring. After identifying the root of problems of their depression, the patient will often find themselves using negative thoughts to dampen positive ones. What this practice does is that it makes the patient write down these negative thoughts then come up with positive ones to counter them. Writing a self-statement and repeating them to yourself when you hear that little negative voice in your head allows you to have a more positive outlook on life. In time, the patient creates new associations that replace the negative thoughts even before they come out. Of course, the statements need not be outrageous or impractical because such yield no results. For example, if the negative thought is 'I am very depressed' saying 'I am very happy' as your positive thought will not yield practical results. However, if instead, you say 'life has its ups and downs and this will not be forever,' you will notice that it is more positive and practical.

The message allows you to be okay with the situation you are currently in and allows you to look forward to what is coming. Explore different statements to convince yourself that life is positive as the same statements can grow old or tired.

10. Progressive muscle relaxation (PMR)

This practice is familiar to those you have dabbled in mindfulness. This technique instructs the patient to relax one muscle group at a time until the whole body enters a state of relaxation. It is best paired with relaxation breathing; you can use audio guidance or even an online video to practice this technique. It is especially useful for people with panic attacks, OCD, and insoothing a busy mind.

Conclusion

According to the three phases of Cognitive Behavioral Therapy, the last step would entail the self-practicing therapy of the patient where they have reached a stage they are able to monitor themselves. This requires discipline and focus. Going forward, the next step would be maintaining commitment and keeping the focus on the goal and keeping this on a feedback loop in order to assist with checking the progress and finding solutions if there is a deviation from the plan in order to make adjustments which are necessary. It could help to have the plan somewhere where it can be easily seen and gone back to periodically. It is not hard to forget the steps which you have set for your transformation. Deadlines can easily be missed if you are not set on your plan. To this effect, you can do a number of things like adding reminders in your diary or on your phone so as to review the plan and tasks. Having a focused attitude also does not mean that you have to be rigid about it.

In reality, things do not usually go according to the plan as one is not able to control everything which can go wrong. It is wise and logical for one to accept those things over which there is no control over and to spend time and energy on the things that you are able to control. It is going to be to your advantage when you accept fallibility as an individual as this is part of the CBT. You can learn to accept the past disappointments and failures and learn to accept the potential of failures in the future and disappointments and exercise control on the way that you choose to react to them. You may choose to respond to the past, present and future adversities with a healthy and rational attitude or with an attitude which is not. The basic thing is as long as you demand that you should be able to control things most of the time and you will be undisturbed when it comes to striving for goals. The basis is to stay focused on the plan and to review the progress which has been made. The reviews allow for feedback on the reality of the situation. You are going to benefit from feedback. It is there to assist you in making decisions in a more confident manner and would allow you to take advantage of opportunities in order to make improvements. You gain feedback when you are studying or the time that you have a performance review coming up at your place of work. This is a significant factor when it comes to learning and developing confidence for success. It would not be wise either to deter from the focus or to ignore scheduled reviews so as to check as to whether you are on target.

www.ingramcontent.com/pod-product-compliance
Lightning Source LLC
Chambersburg PA
CBHW071245070526
44583CB00017B/2328